VILLAGE POST

*Lines from letters
reflecting a century of
change in the
countryside*

England's might is still in her fields and villages, and though the whole weight of mechanised armies roll over them to crush them, in the end they will triumph. The best of England is a village.

CLARENCE HENRY WARREN, 1940.

Lodged deep in most of us is a need for roots and permanence, and the village symbolises a place from which strength and reassurance may be drawn, where the past is always present, neighbourliness is a way of life and where no man needs to be a stranger.

RICHARD MUIR, 1980.

VILLAGE POST

*Lines from letters
reflecting a century of
change in the
countryside*

SORTED BY
KEITH SKIPPER

NOSTALGIA
Publications

TOFTWOOD ○ DEREHAM ○ NORFOLK

Published by:

NOSTALGIA
Publications

(Terry Davy)
7 Elm Park, Toftwood,
Dereham, Norfolk NR19 1NB

First Impression 1996

© Nostalgia Publications 1996

ISBN 0 947630 14 7

Design and Typesetting:
NOSTALGIA PUBLICATIONS

Printed by:
COLOURPRINT
Fakenham, Norfolk

Contents

Acknowledgements

"People tell you so much more in a letter - and it provides excellent microphone material as well as a permanent record."

Those words of wisdom from my earliest days as a broadcaster echoed throughout the mountains I scaled to find fascinating pictures of Norfolk country life this century.

Yes, mountains of mail; but it became a labour of love rather tha a long-winded and onerous chore as about 5,000 letters asked for fresh inspection. I felt more than a twinge of guilt at not being able to include more memories vividly recalled and immacuately written.

The chosen few have to be representative of the prolific many who shared something special along the Village Brantub trail on BBC Radio Norfolk between 1987 and 1994. I'd drop a line to thank them all if only I had time …

Publisher Terry Davy convinced me this project would not be as daunting as 300 bulging blue folders suggested. My wife Diane proved yet again how technology can play a handy part in bringing the good old days to life. Their cheerful and practical support helped me over the deepest furrows.

For grand pictorial support when my own collection fell short I thank: Eastern Counties Newspapers (especially Richard Batson, Bill Smith and Dennis Whitehead), Norfolk Rural Life Museum at Gressenhall, Litcham Historical Society, Clifford Temple, Neil Storey, Terry Davy and two delightful mawthers, Dorothy Scoles and Ena Mason.

My final heartfelt salute to the publishers of Kelly's Directory, 1900 edition, for paving the wonderful way back to the Norfolk villages I love.

Keith Skipper,
Cromer, 1996

Village Memories

- Cowslips on the common.
- Looking down the old well, the bucket on the chain swinging to the middle and back.
- The old black oven in the outside shed.
- The silence when Grandad did his wages book.
- Lying in a huge feather bed with my brother and sister on Christmas Eve petrified as the old oil lamp cast its shadows.
- Granny rolling up the toffee in her hands and cutting it with scissors.
- Grandad lying in his bed after he lost the use of his legs, and everyone coming to see the new television.
- Aunt Florrie looking at the sea rolling in, the word "Interval" coming up on the screen and her saying; "Oh, we'll watch this ... this ought to be good".
- My cousin wearing his mother's silk bloomers on Morston Marshes and having a dip when all was revealed.
- My Uncle's two-string fiddle.
- Grandad's buskins.
- Granny's last words on parting: "Don't let it be so long before you come again."

Heather Dewson (COCKTHORPE)

On the Norfolk trail. Keith Skipper wonders where to head for next in pursuit of mardling and memories

Village Post - First Delivery

I spend much of my time and pocket money in bookshops. It is a wonderful affliction, especially when you have a couple of hours and a few quid to spare along the second-hand shelves.

A tremble of anticipation prefaces every inspection. A triumphant smile greets every fresh discovery or realisation that you can now afford the one you had to leave behind last time. A true sense of satisfaction follows every precious purchase as you willingly thank the person taking your money. Yes, a wonderful affliction. I hope they never find a cure.

I mention my one blatant indulgence simply because it has led to this vibrant chorus of village voices. I also want to remind my wife and sons that I am not talking absolute squit every time I claim another book bought is another useful investment made. In the hope this doesn't sound too much like a desperate bookworm wriggling in a vain attempt to salve his conscience, let me outline the intriguing plot behind Village Post.

On a cold day in the early 1980s I took refuge in a second-hand bookshop in North Norfolk and warmed myself on a fine collection of local volumes. One of them, a Kelly's Norfolk Directory published in 1900, kept me much longer than planned.

The large map "engraved expressly for the work" was missing, and so the asking price had been cut to £15. I just wanted to make sure my old home village of Beeston, the one seven miles west of Dereham, had been afforded proper respect on p46 .... yes, the details were all there from the good old days when the village had three pubs, two grocers, a post office, a castrator and a wheelwright and blacksmith called Henry Cooper, whose gravestone lies horizontally in the churchyard up the hill.

"Purely agricultural, with the houses very much scattered." Well, a bit different on my last journey home, but this was put together nearly a century ago.

The population in 1891 was 469 and there were 71 children at the village school. Now, how many of those names ring a bell? No less than 20 farmers with wheat, barley and turnips the main crops. I wonder how many of those charities are still paid out?

So much to ponder about the shape, size and character of the place where I was born towards the end of the Second World War, a conflict that brought Americans to the aerodrome less than a mile from our village school.

BEESTON (or Beeston-next-Mileham) is a large and pleasant village standing on high ground, 2 miles north from the Fransham station on the Lynn branch of the Great Eastern railway and 7 west from Dereham, in the Mid division of the county, Launditch hundred, Mitford and Launditch petty sessional division and union, Dereham county court district, rural deanery of South Brisley, archdeaconry of Lynn and diocese of Norwich; it is purely agricultural, with the houses very much scattered. For civil purposes it is united with Bittering Parva, which is ecclesiastically a separate parish, the civil parish being known as Beeston with Little Bittering. The church of St. Mary is a building of flint with stone dressings, in the Early Decorated style, consisting of chancel with chapel, clerestoried nave of four bays, aisles, north porch, and an embattled western tower with spire, containing one bell: the tower was struck by lightning and burnt down in May, 1872, and rebuilt in 1873: in the church is a finely carved screen: there are 200 sittings. The register dates from the year 1538. The living is a rectory, net yearly value £276, including 30 acres of glebe, with residence, in the gift of the trustees of the late John Twoffield Orton, and held since 1895 by the Rev. Thomas Willis Butler Bartlett, of St. Bees, who is also vicar of Kempston. The rectory house, formerly surrounded by a moat, which has been filled in on one side, was burnt down in the reign of James I. and rebuilt on the same site. Here is a Primitive Methodist chapel. The charities include the church land of 8 acres 15 perches, let for £9; the rector's dole of £1; Huke's charity, £5 for the poor and to the rector £1 for preaching a Good Friday sermon; Halcott's charity of £2 8s. for bread, to be distributed every sunday; Alee's charity of £1 12s. given away in bread; Gooch's charity (1634), ranging from £2 16s. to £4 8s. and given to the poor in money; a fuel allotment of 20 acres, rented at £27, and the Clay Pit allotment let at £1 6s. which sum is distributed in coals. Henry Edward Paine esq. is lord of the manor. William Thomas Collison esq. of Albemarle House, Yarmouth, Robert Harvey Mason esq. of Necton Hall, Miss Hoste, the trustees of the late C. Wallis esq. and Mrs. Stedman, of Wood Hill, Gressenhall, are the principal landowners. The soil is light loam and clay; subsoil, gravel and clay. The chief crops are wheat, barley and turnips. The area is 2,502 acres; rateable value, £2,133; the population in 1891 was 469.

Parish Clerk, James Head.

Post Office.—Mrs. Eliza Preston, sub-postmistress. Letters arrive through Swaffham at 8 a.m. & 5.25 p.m.; dispatched at 9.30 a.m. & 5.30 p.m. Postal orders are issued here, but not paid. Wall Letter Box, cleared at 9.40 a.m. & 5.45 p.m. & 8.40 a.m. sundays. Litcham is the nearest money order & telegraph office, 3 miles distant

A School Board of five members was formed July 14, 1875, for Beeston All Saints & Little Bittering; W. L. Regester, of Great Dunham, clerk to the board

Board School (mixed), built in 1879, at a cost of £850, for 71 children; average attendance, 68; Albert Victor Jordan, master

Bartlett Rev. Thomas Willis Butler, Rectory
Dowling Edward
Preston James

COMMERCIAL.

Archer James, farmer, Bell hall
Bell Mary Ann (Miss), farmer
Bolton Edward, farmer, New farm
Bolton William Jennings (exors. of), farmers, Manor farm (postal address, Litcham)
Buscall Charles, farmer

Claxton Henry, castrator
Claxton Robert, farmer
Claxton William, farmer
Cooper Hy. wheelwright & blacksmith
Culley John, farmer
Frost Charles, farmer
Gapp Henry, draper & grocer
Gunton Jn. Percy, Holkham ArmsP.H
Hart George, farmer
Holman Robert Palmer, farmer
Linford George, farmer
Mitchell William Saunders, farmer

Orton John, farmer
Parke Frederick, farmer
Rivett Henry, farmer & landowner
Sculpher Geo. Dennis, farmer, Conway farm (letters address Mileham)
Starling Jas. farmer (postal address, Litcham)
Stibbon Ann (Mrs.), farmer
Vince William C. farmer
Vincent John, Bell P.H
Ward Walter George, grocer
Wyett Henry, Ploughshare P.H

Extract from Kelly's Directory of 1900 - the starting point for "Village Post"

The school is still there, although numbers have fallen to worrying levels, but there are different kinds of wings on the runway that leads into Wendling. Turkeys in sheds instead of bombers with painted ladies on the side.

Fransham railway station, where I caught the train to grammar school in Swaffham, has long been closed. Mitford and Launditch Rural District Council is just another minute in the history of local government. The Methodist chapel where we recited and sang with such gusto on Sunday School anniversaries was knocked down years ago. You have to look carefully now to find a farm worker ...

A catalogue of big changes in my lifetime, let alone since this directory was published. I turned to a few other villages close to the old homestead, Litcham, Longham, Mileham, Tittleshall. I let the process repeat itself. A pub gone there, a shop closed here. That family is still about, but the farm has a different name. More people there now thanks to that new estate. Wonder if their workers' bus still runs? And what about that industrial area they planned near the council houses?

I soon convinced myself these matters were of considerable importance as we embarked on the final lap of the century. Yes, many of the new villagers flocking to Norfolk were retired or destined to be instant commuters, and some places were being transformed into large and colourless dormitories. (The development boom was in full cry).

Even so, the true rural spirit had to survive, and this "bible" could help spread the gospel!

It was with such evangelical fervour that I handed over £15 and took possession of a book destined to play a major part in my life for well over a decade. I still find regular refreshment in its pages.

In my role as presenter and producer of Radio Norfolk's Dinnertime Show for nearly 15 years, broadcasting each weekday from a studio I called Cell 33, I worked overtime to get to "the heart of the county." This meant a lot of attention for hundreds of villages in the listening area, many of them well beyond the influence of an ever-sprawling city and all its urban habits.

Fortunately, I knew well most of the communities regularly in the spotlight, contacts made during my years on the local Press and more recent invitations to attend various functions in village hall, pub or school maintaining old links and forging new ones. My own village background clearly helped establish a useful rapport with far-flung corners of the Norfolk empire.

It was evident, however, that even more could be done to draw timely attention to the rapidly changing face of country life. Working on the reasonable basis that you can't see where you might be going unless you have a shrewd idea where you have been, I turned to Kelly's Norfolk Directory of 1900. I just knew it would come in useful.

The scheme was to condense nearly a hundred years into a few hours, featuring a different village each week and inviting 'phone calls, letters and visits to the studio by residents old and new.

This potted local history exercise began in October, 1987. It ended nearly 300 villages later in October, 1994. Responses varied. Wintry weather, harvest duties, family commitments, failed MOT's and misplaced dentures were among reasons given for much-regretted absences from live Friday get-togethers, but it proved one of the most popular items on our local airwaves.

There were three stages. On Monday I asked for 'phone calls after painting a picture of our featured village at the turn of the century from Kelly's Directory. Were some of the names and trades still in fashion? I wanted to hear from listeners who were born there, grew up there or had stayed there to see dramatic changes over the years. If fact, any connections at all … "You may be on the parish council, run the post office or village pub. Perhaps you used to teach at the little school or attend it 50 or 60 years ago. Don't forget to share all those marvellous characters and funny stories!.

"What sort of place is it today and are there any big plans for the future? It doesn't matter if you have been there for two months or 80 years, give us a ring and tell us what you know and what you think."

At the end of the Monday session I called for letters, not least from those who had 'phoned with memories and details of what was going on these days at the playgroup and village hall. Now they had a chance to put a bit more flesh on those rural bones and to prompt relations and friends to get in touch as well.

On many occasions people who lived way beyond Norfolk's boundaries were alerted to the fact that "their village" was being featured, and they responded eagerly with graphic accounts of childhood days in a county still very close to their hearts. A select few were able to make the long journey back for a mardle and that could mean tears of joy as the memories flowed.

Wednesday's programme brought the second stage into play and it was often a case of squeezing a quart into a pint pot as a dozen or more packed letters demanded full attention.

The picture was building up the whole time, especially when letters were accompanied by family albums, scrapbooks, village histories and the latest edition of the church newsletter.

Some had intimated readiness to pay a visit to the studio when they rang at the start of the week. Others made it plain in their letters that they would be happy to join the throng if needed. Naturally, we gave priority to volunteers, but always taking care to present as wide a cross-section of interests as possible.

About 2000 people made Brantub visits to Norfolk Tower, some of them gleefully admitting it was their first trip to Norwich in years. Old school chums were reunited before going on air, retired teachers met pupils they had not seen since before the war and members of the same village cricket team enjoyed an innings together for the first time in decades.

Sometimes nostalgic cosiness gave way to a spot of controversy over the way the village had developed, although I took pains to explain the laws of slander before the microphones were switched on! Village memories go back a long way.

I was lost for words but once when a twinkling rogue of a rustic had the perfect Norfolk answer to a question that would pass as straightforward in most other places;

"Tell me, have you lived in the village all your life?" "No not yet I hent!"

There were no rehearsals and no strict rules after the cautionary words about slander and profanities. The vast majority excelled with affectionate banter, shrewd advice, colourful anecdotes and real pride in representing their parish.

I jotted down my top ten of the most often-used remarks, either on air or in letters;

- *"I walk round the place these days and I hardly know a soul".*
- *"We had to make our own amusement."*
- *"I'm a newcomer - only been there 25 years".*
- *"You don't get the characters like you used to."*

Cley from the sky … nestling by the sea in North Norfolk

- *"If the local bobby boxed your ears you daren't tell your parents in case you got another one."*
- *"Life was hard, but we all helped each other."*
- *"Yes, we did get up to some tricks, but there was never any malice."*
- *"I don't think getting the cane did me any harm."*
- *"We had to go to chapel three times every Sunday."*
- *"Some of the new people have mucked in."*

Memory can be most selective, and distance has been known to lend a little enchantment, but there does seem to have been a comforting sureness, an easier blending of the human and natural worlds, a deeper attachment to one place whatever its limitations, in the Norfolk of just 30 or 40 years back.

Many who spoke or wrote to me about village life had left it, for various reasons, some considerable time before and their views were bound to be coated in nostalgia. Their predictable worries about today and tomorrow were based to some degree on what they remembered or had heard rather than on first-hand experience.

Of those in the "village stalwart" category, inhabitants of the same place for 50 years or longer, a fair number were happy to admit to genuine improvements in recent time, especially in housing, sanitation and sports facilities. Even so, they could all point too often to a sad decline in local services, some villages losing shop, pub, chapel, school, bus service and all but a few traces of the old-fashioned brand of togetherness.

They saw commuting newcomers driving off to work each morning, children board a bus to the nearest school four or five miles away and lonely fields where dozens of men used to ebb and flow with the rhythms of the seasons.

On the credit side they could herald a new community centre or extended village hall and a successful fund-raising drive for vital repairs to the parish church. Even where they had to share a clergyman with half a dozen other parishes there appeared to be healthy backing for the idea of the church remaining at the core of local activities.

In the same way that I knew the 1900 directory would be a valuable asset long before my brantub idea emerged, so I happily accepted the need to store away over 5,000 letters for a form of "permanent recycling" one day.

Village Post, with 11 sections, stretched my editorial resources to the limit even if many of the letters did deal with the same topic or expressed similar sentiments. I was spoilt for choice and forced to adopt the sort of ruthless streak that prompts a heady mixture of power and regret.

Those who claim I have more than one foot planted in the past must acknowledge the inclusion of a final chapter devoted to enthusiasts, some of them newcomers, who want to underline the amount of good work going on in our villages today. I am definitely not sounding the Last Post.

Pictures have been carefully selected to complement a host of village voices. I listened to them afresh with gratitude after a privileged seven-year journey

The horse-drawn honeycart makes slow but sure progress through the snow

beginning at Hales, near Loddon, and ending at Castle Rising only a few days after that most delightful of places near King's Lynn had collected plaudits in the Best-Kept Village Competition.

A romantic notion, I suppose, but perhaps a faded copy of Village Post will be coaxed down from a dusty shelf in a Norfolk second-hand bookshop in about 70 or 80 years time to fire new enthusiasms for the old debate.

They'll ask if they really were the good old days before telecottages, satellite shopping and gardening by 'phone. The search will be on for someone who actually used an out-of-town supermarket for enough supplies to last a month. Experts will strive to locate the one settlement where a bypass was never built.

And whatever happened to the honeycart?

From Dawn till Dusk

It wasn't until about three decades ago that Norfolk villages fully accepted the sun was setting on the old agricultural scene. Mechanisation and capital started to dominate instead of labour.

A single man was employed where half a dozen or more had been needed. The disappearance of the heavy horse put hosts of saddlers, harness-makers and wheelwrights out of work.

Changes on the land gave village life a completely new character, much of the continuity and self-sufficiency running through the first half of the century vanishing over the headlands. Suddenly, the bulk of people living in a village had nothing directly to do with work on the farm.

That work had meant long hours and wages scarcely stretching beyond the bare needs of subsistence. Stations in country life were largely accepted. As the farmworker had no real opportunity for self-enhancement, he accepted his lot however unjust and taxing it may have been.

For all that, memories of hard graft from dawn till dusk do carry a gentle edge, not least because every workforce, including those in the fishing village clinging to the coastline, contained people of considerable sensitivity and ability.

Perhaps the fact that the corn harvest was the closest many of them came to the time of plenty has coloured views from the world of horses, binders and boys with sticks waiting for rabbits. But there can be no denying the strong feeling of community when it came to gathering in the sheaves. It was a real family effort.

This selection of extracts from letters sets the trend for all subsequent chapters. The village in brackets after the writer's name indicates the location for memories and details being shared; the writer may not necessarily still live there, or have been a resident at any time.

I was only four years old when we moved to Alburgh but I can remember taking the dinners to the harvest field. I always think of runner beans as harvest food as they were one of the main vegetables for the dinners with rabbit pie and the bottles of tea wrapped in a newspaper and pushed in old socks to keep it warm.

Ivy Harris (ALBURGH)

We lived at Foresters Farm and at the back of the house was a square thatched building, just one storey and thick clay lump walls. It had windows, just holes in the wall, covered with perforated zinc inside and slats outside. This was the dairy and the pails of warm straight-from-the-cow milk were brought in and put into big brown crocks. Rennet was added to make farmhouse cheese. Some of the milk was set out in large shallow bowls and left to get cold so that the cream could be taken off to make butter. It was always cool and had that distinctive smell of old-time dairies ... no strong disinfectant then.

Beryl Smith (BEDINGHAM)

Cats waiting for a treat as work in the dairy gathers pace

I took over Home Farm from Colonel Sir Edmund Neville in 1961, a bit over 500 acres, with the existing staff of nine. At that time the farm had four small tractors, two jobbing horses and a tractor-drawn Ransome's combine that on a good day could just manage six acres. We began to diversify into vining peas and potatoes and at that time two tons of wheat, 12 tons of potatoes and 30cwt. of barley were respectable yields and how we managed to find work for all nine men is now difficult to remember. What is easy to remember is the loading of vining peas on to trailers with the help of an "Imitation Waddling Duck" rear loader and much hard work running into the night.

Robin Sayer (SLOLEY)

*W*hen I first came here in 1952 heavy horses were still in use for some farm jobs and often there was one tied to a plum tree near the house during the lunch hour. This horse, Thomas, was always being told off for putting his big feet on the plants while "hoss hoeing" the sugar beet. We had weekly delivery calls from two butchers, two grocers, a baker and a fishman as well as a daily milkman. We had no car at first and had to bike everywhere. We had no mains water either; water came from a well and a large rain water tank. Cattle were still being driven along the main road to the marshes near Wayford Bridge and often they got into the gardens on the way. Our front lawn suffered several times.

Joan Harmer (SMALLBURGH)

*J*oe Strike worked on Grange Farm when I was a boy. I used to do a harvest which lasted about five weeks. One fourses time I aggravated Joe so much he got a plough line and tied me to a post so he could have his food in peace. At five years old I sat on a box in the centre and kept the horse, Captain, going round and round to operate the elevator. After that I was a holdgee boy. For my first harvest I got £1 for five weeks, good pay in those days.

Fred Calver (SMALLBURGH)

*M*y grandfather and father both worked at Wortwell Mill, grandfather driving the miller's cart and delivering flour as far afield as Elmswell bacon factory. My father, Bob Calver, carried on the tradition. My parents ran the mill from 1926 until 1944. If my father wasn't sure which was plain flour and which was self-raising, it was brought into the house for mother to taste. As a young girl I would hang these huge sacks of corn on chains to be hoisted to the top of the mill.

Maureen Potter (WORTWELL)

Lots of the village women used to go cockling. You could stand at the bottom of Holly Lane and see them on the strand looking for all the world like a flock of feeding ostriches I saw out in the East African bush. The cockles were carried down to the bottom of the marsh where they were put on pony carts. Some went to the station at Wells and some were hawked round the adjoining villages. The marshes were a great playground and larder for children. We spent hours there, fishing in the creeks for butts, gathering samphire and searching the tangle to see what had been washed up on the last tide.

Bill Claxton (STIFFKEY)

During my childhood in the 1920s I can remember cycling to Yarmouth on Sunday mornings to see the men off in the drifters. I recall the warehouses where women and girls mended the nets and the old stone at the bottom of the lane where the old men sat and had a mardle. The fishermen smoked their pipes in the sheds on the beach. We were afraid to go in but peeped in the door. You couldn't see for smoke and the smell was terrible. I also recall the shrimps my grandfather caught. The table was scrubbed, the boiling pots brought out and the dishes piled high from the folk around with little notes of one or two pints. Grandfather was called Old Roger.

Ella Emmerson (WINTERTON)

My father worked for the Mann family from the age of 11 when he went scaring rooks and picking stones. He worked on the Grange Farm until he retired at 65 and went to live in the Memorial Cottages built by the Mann family in memory of a son killed in the First World War. Dad kept working, sweeping the hall drive and making sure it was tidy, until he was 81. On December 20th every year the schoolchildren marched to Thelveton Hall on Miss Molly Mann's birthday and were given a book, a meat patty, a bun, an apple and an orange. Miss Molly was Sir John's sister.

Winnie Bloomfield (THELVETON)

The most exciting place was the harvest field where we would ride on the horses pulling the carts laden with sheaves to the elevator. The horses worked in pairs, Bruiser and Blossom and Toby and Punch. Many a long sunny day would I ride on Bruiser's back. My legs, not long enough to reach the shafts, would be caked with a combination of chaff, dirt and grease. But this did not deter me and I became quite proficient.

Anne Webster (BODNEY)

Harvest "chariot" cuts into the crop at Edgefield while horses pull towards the headland.

My father, James Haylock, was a team-man earning ten shillings a week. He later became a pork butcher and baker. Most people kept a pig in those days, and father would go round to kill them. He took his killing stool with him. I left school when the First World War broke out, and at 13 I looked after sheep on Carbrooke fen. A year later I started to plough with horses pulling a wooden implement. If the plough fell over I was too small to lift it up again!

Harry Haylock (CARBROOKE)

My memories of our summer holidays centre on my mother cooking beef puddings, rabbit stew and dumplings with vegetables and gravy. We took a hot meal which my sisters and I enjoyed in the harvest field with Dad. We returned home with the empty dishes and after a while set off again with bottles of drink and the fourses. Dad worked from dawn until dusk and Mother worked just as hard. We had no electricity so she had to do all the cooking over a coal fire

Norah Brindid (EAST RUSTON)

Two tradesmen of the 1940s were Curly Taylor the blacksmith and Bob Lansdell the wheelwright. They had their shops adjacent to the village school. Most nights we would stand and watch Curly shoeing the massive horses. Curly, a little man,.... swearing, sweating, swearing, heaving, swearing and pushing those large horses around and the distinctive smell of the hot shoe being fitted to the hoof. And Bob Lansdell making large wooden wheels for wagons of the day. Bob always said he made them "by eye" using only a spokeshave. Unbelievable! Every now and again the two would co-operate to rim a wooden wheel. We watched in amazement as it was placed on the pad on the ground and the red hot rim made by Curly was placed over the wheel. After the stinking steam from the iron and wood had cleared, we beheld a perfectly fitted rim and a perfectly fitted wheel. Two perfect tradesmen.

Neville Day (HEMPNALL)

Men and boys tackle threshing time - and the dog is ready for a spot of sport when the rats come out!

My father Jack Wymer was known as the Raspberry King. He collected them from all the growers in the area to take them to Braceys of Martham, who then sent them off to the jam factories. Nearly everyone in the village grew raspberries.

Marjorie Cheriton (FILBY)

My parents Robert and Lily Wright were cowman and dairymaid at Home Farm, working for Sir Maurice Boileau and, after his death, for Sir Raymond and Lady Boileau. After milking, my father would put his churn on a three-wheel trike along with his pint and half-pint measures. We all had our own mugs at school and Father would fill them to the brim, much to the annoyance of teacher Mrs. Limmer. I spent many hours separating milk and making butter to help my mother. (This butter was for the Hall.) Villagers would bring jugs or cans to collect skimmed milk at a penny a pint.

Daphne Frarey (KETTERINGHAM)

My dad worked on the railway as a fireman. He started working as a cleaner in 1910, and in 1936 he moved to Peterborough to get a regular driver's job. At Melton Constable he was driving during the summer months and firing through the winter. While he was at Melton he became secretary of the improvement class for young men just learning the job. They used to meet on Sunday mornings as there were no trains on that day except during the summer months when there were excursions to Sheringham and Cromer.

Brenda Sutherland (MELTON CONSTABLE)

I took over Dairy Farm on the death of my father in 1959. By 1965 a lot of the land was being lost to developments, such as the new school and sewage works. By 1972, with a shrinking farm and a growing family, we reluctantly decided we would have to move to a larger set up. To me and my family North Wootton will always be home. We go back as often as we can to see the views to the Wash. It must be one of the best places on the map with birds of foreshore, inland marsh, farmland, woodland and heath all in one village.

Alfred Graver (NORTH WOOTTON)

Grandad Jarvis had a very hard life as a woodman, going off with a pack of victuals on his back and often being away for days at a time. Being unable to read or write, he used to notch up his working hours on a tree trunk and received his pittance of pay every six months. Disaster struck once when the ownership changed hands and he lost six months pay because he could not produce evidence of his work other than the notches on the trunk. However, by that time some of the older ones were at work and all rallied round to keep the family going. We have often wondered how they managed such a large family in such a small house known by the younger generation, jokingly but lovingly, as Mud Hall.

Peggy Howell (BEDINGHAM)

*A*s a small boy in the 1930s I recall staying with Aunt Violet Hipkin. I remember men and older boys with sticks, watching and waiting for rabbits to run from the path of the binder in the harvest field. Then there was the time I was lifted on to the back of a horse for a ride back to the village. On a warm summer evening I had to be scrubbed clean by Aunt Violet; this operation took place by the back door of the cottage, very handy for the soft water butt!

Stan Langley (TOTTENHILL)

*S*everal events spring to mind from the late 1920s. Like carting water for the threshing machine from the river at Larling Ford with horse and three-wheeled water cart and cutting bracken on the heath for bedding cattle in the winter. This was done with two horses pulling a sailer, an old type of machine used to cut corn before the binder was invented. All the farmers in Larling carted sugar beet to Harling Road Station, loaded by hand into rail trucks bound for Bury sugar factory.

Tom Larwood (LARLING)

Busy times for the miller at Wreningham

23

Rhubarb harvest at Syderstone in the 1920s. It was taken by horse and cart to Hunstanton to sell.

No less than three local farmers sold their milk door to door - Mr. King, Mrs. Laws and the Hammond brothers who carried the milkchurns on their cycle handlebars. The Morleys sold the best bread I have ever tasted and no child sent to fetch the bread left without a sweet or an apple.

Pat Offley (FINCHAM)

In the late 1940s most of the farm work was still being done with horses. As the horse-drawn binder completed the cutting of a field there were lots of boys with sticks ready to knock down a rabbit. They were all laid out and then shared. I remember how proud and pleased I was when I had one to take home.

Philip Meakings (AYLMERTON)

My grandfather, Herbert Wink, was gamekeeper at Oxnead from 1931 for about 35 years. He came from Rackheath but was still working for the same employer, a Mr. Edward Stracey. I spent some days as a boy in the summer holidays with my grandfather and we would go and check the traps. Then he would take me to Burgh Cock or Brampton Maid's Head for a pint.

Michael Abbs (OXNEAD)

The Happiest Days . . .

The most intriguing aspect of letters about days at the village school was the number of former teachers who felt the urge to prove their joined up writing remained in fine fettle! In many cases of course, they taught two or three generations of the same family in the same school and so felt particularly close to a community at the centre of their working life.

Even those pupils who confessed to being a few slates short of educational excellence or, in a few outstanding cases, worthy of any punishment meted out showed healthy powers of recall when it came to their teachers' names. Then, perhaps, they had more reason to remember.

Our exercise books of experience are crammed with similar stories - a curtain dividing one class from another; milk thawing in front of the coke fire; a Christmas concert punctuated by little accidents; painful visits to the school dentist parked in his van in the playground; daft diversions on the way home.

At a time when many of our smaller village schools are still under threat for strictly economic reasons, we point to our own early schooldays as evidence of the value of fashioning that precious sense of belonging. Places where schools have closed must find it difficult to attract young families. The retired and career hungry commuters must dominate, while any children there are forced to travel by bus or car to a bigger school some miles away.

Yes, there is much more than sentiment attached to schoolday memories. Important social arguments will continue to arise from inevitable comparisons between yesterday and today.

My arithmetic began with little white shells for counting, adding and dividing and we had slates and slate pencils to write with. The Rector came to school quite often and we had to recite the Catechism or the 23rd Psalm and he said prayers before he left. He was the Rev. Cubison and he christened my sister Bessie in 1918 with water from the River Jordan.

Dorothy Johnson (ASHMANHAUGH)

Divided classroom - but undivided attention at Great Ryburgh School

I went to the village school until I was 15. Miss Kate Lancaster was the infant teacher and she took my trousers down and walloped me with a short, stiff brush. I can't remember what I did but I expect I deserved it. The toilets had a door on the back for "burying the donkey" and legend has it that Wally Tingay opened it and stung the teacher on the backside with a nettle. Another young rascal was Ray Day who put Bessie Carter's umbrella on the flagpole right at the top of the church.

Charlie Sharpin (GOODERSTONE)

As we had no primary school I attended Burgh School. To get there we had to cross three bridges, all over water. One was over a dyke, one over the River Bure and the other over the Mermaid. This was at the bottom of a steep hill near Hall Farm. One morning I was going down the hill on my little blue bike and I couldn't stop. I managed to jump off but caught my toe in a broken plank and went headfirst into the muddy Mermaid. Good job Mum was there. She shouted loud enough so Leslie Thompson, a cowman at Hall Farm, heard her and helped to pull me out. Freezing cold I was taken home for a bath by the fire and put to bed but this is not recommended as an excuse for a seven year old to have a day off school.

Jenny Cole (BRAMPTON)

The school was built in 1850. All the children were taught together in one room but the tiny playground was divided into two, half for boys and half for girls. The last teacher at the school was Miss Barbara Samples. She cycled every day from Hindringham, 14 miles each way, to teach the last five children. The school closed on April 12th, 1922, with local children moving on to Lyng.

Grace Gaff (SPARHAM)

In our last year at school we often had to teach lads our age to read. One I used to help put his hand up at the start of class one morning. Teacher said "Yes?". He said "How do you spell Wennsday?" She replied; "PLEASE". And so his days work was headed PLEASE, 14th May, 1935.

Dusty Miller (HEVINGHAM)

I did my first teaching practice at the school while I was training at Keswick Hall. When I went home I said how fitting it was that my headteacher was a Miss Regester - proper Happy Families name - and my mother immediately pricked up her ears. She said there had been a Doris Regester in her group when she was at college in Norwich ... and it turned out to be the same person.

Josephine Thompson (DICKLEBURGH)

Youngsters at Lexham in mid-Norfolk take a break from classes in the early part of the century

Palgrave pupils and teachers outside the village school in South Norfolk

J taught at Aldborough School for 23 years until I retired in 1981. The school is really in Alby, and in my days there children from 11 parishes attended. The highest number I can recall was 121 after the closure of Wickmere School. The winter highlight was the Christmas concert when each of the four classes acted a play, the choir boys and girls sang their very best and the school band played their instruments with gusto. Oh, happy, happy days! I could cry!

Betty Crouch (ALDBOROUGH)

J well remember my first day at school. We were taken into the classroom and told to stand in a circle while we said prayers. I had a quick look round, saw everyone had got their eyes shut and promptly disappeared out of the door. I was back three quarters of an hour later having received a good ding of the lug!

Bob Warnes (CARBROOKE)

J was the infant teacher there from 1931 to 1939, my first school after training. It was the time of severe cuts when all civil servants, police, teachers etc. had to take a 10 per cent cut twice in the one year. This was in 1931 and, oh dear, was I hard up!

Constance Boyce (HAPTON)

28

I was born and brought up in Holme Hale and I am very proud of the fact that I hold the record for longest attendance at the village school. I started at the age of four and a half and stayed on until I was 16. I became a school manager and held that post until the school was closed.

Bob Doudy (HOLME HALE)

I remember visiting the school dentist in a caravan in the school yard. Having taken home the dreaded form, and getting it signed by a parent, when your name was called out you marched bravely out of the classroom and up the steps of the van where the dreaded dental smell assailed your nostrils. But how brave you felt when you exposed the gap on meeting your friends. No badges for bravery in those days!

Mary Hylton (CRANWORTH)

I started school when I was five in 1941 and the headmistress at the village seat of learning on the common was Mrs. Rowbottom, a lovely lady and a teacher of the "old school". There were about 72 pupils and a green curtain divided the juniors from the seniors. Miss Larner was the junior teacher and made sure there was no hanky-panky with the other side of the curtain. Mrs. Nicholls was the infant teacher and I can remember her singing "All Things Bright and Beautiful" as she dusted the classroom first thing in the morning. I also recall the awful milk placed in front of the fire in winter. Bottles nearest the fire were "cooked" while those on the other side of the crate were still frozen.

Brenda Ford (MULBARTON)

I started school at Topcroft two miles away at the age of four-and-a-half. We had to walk unless we were lucky enough to cadge a ride on the back of somebody's bike. I was obviously a hooligan in the making because a few months after starting school I disgraced myself on the way home by having a fight with a girl from nearby Denton who was also at Topcroft School. Not only did we fight but I peed all over her brand new bicycle. After heated meetings between parents we were both expelled from Topcroft. I was sent to Woodton and she went to Denton. Strangely enough, three years later her parents took over Foresters Farm when we left and became our near neighbours. The families became friends. We still keep in touch and enjoy a laugh over those childhood incidents.

Neville Nobbs (BEDINGHAM)

How many can you recognise in this early 1940s photograph of Whinburgh school pupils?

My father, William Challoner, was headmaster of the village school from 1933 until his retirement in 1968. My mother Dulcie, whom he met while they were both pupils at Ashmanhaugh School, was also a qualified teacher and joined my father at the school in 1948, retiring in 1966. The school had an excellent and dedicated staff, most notably Mrs. Annie Easton who attended first as a pupil, then pupil teacher, then certificated teacher (after the 1945 Act), finally retiring in the early 1950s after 50 years attendance!

Roger Challoner (NEATISHEAD)

I spent several happy years teaching before I was married in 1929. I cycled to Nordelph School from Downham Market every day. They came from families of very hard workers, and as the children helped their parents on the land the summer holidays were split up. We had a month's holiday for strawberry picking, returned to school and then had another month off later for the potato crop. The children knew how their holidays were going to be spent and they certainly earned their pocket money in those days.

Margery English (NORDELPH)

Home-made Fun

Many of today's youngsters find it hard to imagine life without television and videos. They automatically flick on a switch or press a button in pursuit of instant entertainment. They laugh long and loud when the older generation mutter about times when you had to make your own amusement ....

Well, before television took its grip on the domestic scene a trip to the pictures was a big event. I recall the travelling cinema man coming to our old village hall, a Nissen hut on the aerodrome, for Friday night with George Formby, The Little Rascals, Tom Mix and other favourites on his magic reels. The adventures were given another whirl in the school playground on Monday if the projector hadn't broken down and left us in the dark.

There was more room for imagination and invention. Village socials and concert parties were the high points of communal culture, the parson playing opposite the roadmender and the teacher helping the cowman along in a manner befitting the creator of a minor masterpiece of dramatic content. Happily, there appears to be a revival on this stage, not least with widespread support for the village pantomime.

Cricket and football teams used to wear distinctly local colours before car ownership ushered in a different attitude to club loyalties. Pub entertainment didn't come from a juke box or any other flashing machine; Billy would give you a tune on the accordion and Ethel was always good for a song on Saturday night.

The world was smaller. Demands were simpler. And home-made fun was all the sweeter for knowing exactly where it came from.

I spent the whole of my young life at Tasburgh, and as there was no bus service to Norwich we had to make our own amusements. My father was Rector and we used to hold socials, concerts and even plays in the school at the bottom of the Rectory garden. We also had a pierrot troupe which went round the villages making money for charity. During the war the Rectory was taken over by the Irish Guards on manoeuvre. There were gun emplacements all over the garden and we had to show our identity cards before they would let us into our own house!

Shirley Gates (TASBURGH)

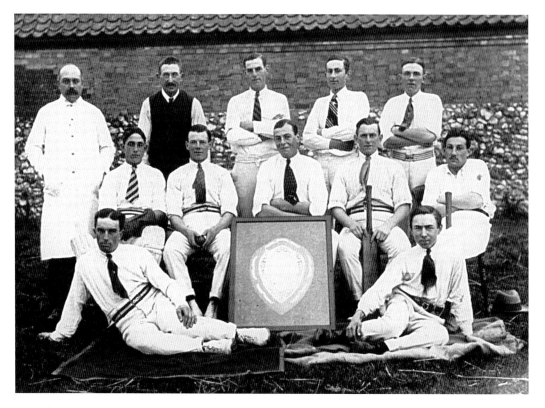

Stanfield and Mileham cricket team from the 1920s. Back row (left to right): William Pigg (umpire), Sidney Hart, Frank Kemp, Billy Cason, Joe Cason; Middle row: Norman Dye, Dick Goderson, Herbert Kemp, James Goderson, Monty Mills; Front row: Harold Riches, Albert Webster

During the last war a mobile cinema would come to Catfield village hall. About a dozen of us boys and girls from Potter Heigham would walk the two miles on a Tuesday evening to see Hopalong Cassidy, Roy Rogers and other favourites. We would have been only 10 or 11 at the time - but could we let our children do that in this age?

Mervyn Hinton (CATFIELD)

Major Henry Birkbeck had a private family cricket square on the park at Westacre High House. I used to keep sheep on the park in the 1930s. At that time there were four or five gardeners at the Hall and one of them would keep the cricket square in tip-top condition with a motor mower and heavy roller. If the sheep accidentally soiled the sacred turf, the droppings, when dry, were cleaned up by shovel and bucket and taken into the gardens for fertiliser.

Jeff Rye (WESTACRE)

$\mathcal{S}$tibbard Band was formed in 1921 by my grandfather, John Abram, who was the local publican, newsagent and milk haulier. The Band achieved a good contest record and developed several excellent players. It was disbanded on the outbreak of war but re-formed in 1948 using the original instruments and uniforms. By that time my father had taught me to play. Every evening seemed to be a musical evening in our house with Dad on euphonium and me on cornet. Mother never complained!

Brian Abram (STIBBARD)

$\mathcal{T}$he Jubilee and Coronation celebrations of 1930s brought jollifications to the village. There was a fete and sports and plenty of food. We children decorated our dolls' prams and bikes. I remember the men ran from Whitwell Hall to the Goat Inn, downed a pint, moved on to the Black Horse for another pint and then toiled up the hill towards the finishing line. I recall seeing them stretched out, panting, and most of them in a state of collapse.

June Hannant (SKEYTON)

A pillow fight for grown-ups at Swanton Abbott Gala in the 1930s

Bowls enthusiasts of all ages at Burnham Market in 1936

*O*ur cricket ground was a most delightful place in a beautiful setting with Smallburgh Hall in the background. My father, Harold Neave, played there for East Norfolk. I watched many of the matches and can remember a team captained by my father when Bill Edrich was playing. During the war the ground was used for fixtures between the local Home Guard and Army and RAF personnel stationed in the area. It seemed like a sin when the ground was ploughed up due to food shortages immediately after the war, although the pavilion was moved to the old playing field and used as the village hall for a few years.

Joan Harmer (SMALLBURGH)

*T*he village at one time had thriving cricket and football teams. My father and uncle both played cricket and had to cycle to the farm in the tea interval, milk the cows and then rush back to the match! I used to score for the team and enjoyed trips by coach to other villages for contests on various nettle and thistle-clad pitches, not to mention cow pats and rabbit holes to catch the unwary players.

Jean Dack (SCARNING)

The characters I remember most from the Hempnall cricket team in the 1950s were the Downing boys Herbert and Charlie. Mrs. Downing would sit on the edge of the field with us, the visiting team. "My boy, Harbet, he'll git a hundred terday" she would say and more often than not, he would. Then there was fast bowler Penn. He stood about seven feet tall and as he bowled up the slope we batsmen never really saw him until he was at the wicket. We had reason to believe he started his run-up in the next field. The thought of him pounding in was enough to make tailenders' knees and teeth create sufficient noise to drown out the sounds of the countryside.

Keith Saunders (HEMPNALL)

I remember how we children organised a concert during the summer holidays. We were allowed to rehearse in the school and opening night in the Reading Room saw us perform in front of a full house. We raised £50 and it was decided to take all the old-age pensioners on a coach trip along the coast, starting at Sheringham and ending up in Yarmouth for tea. One dear lady, Emily Plumber, had never been out of the village. So this was quite an adventure for her as she was in her 80s at the time.

Dianne Capocci (RINGLAND)

Hingham Minstrels are ready to entertain

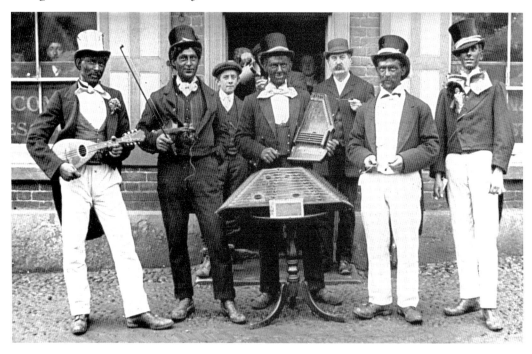

*I*n the late 1940s we had girl's keep-fit classes every Monday night with my sister, Joan, as the leader. It was old-time dancing on Tuesdays with MC Harry Dorran and Mrs. Dorran of Hemsby and Yvonne at the piano. These classes were held in the old Institute which was also a meeting place for boys from the surrounding villages. Many found their future husbands there - including me!

Janet Partridge (MARTHAM)

*I*n 1950 two ladies by the name of Dorrie Scott and Marjorie Brown formed a gym club, ages ranging from eight to 13. It was great fun and eventually the girls gave concerts in the pavilion in aid of church funds. These events were always well supported and many will remember with affection The Grassy Green Theatre.

Wendy Wills (ROYDON, NEAR DISS)

*M*usic has played a big part in my life as my father played the concertina and my mother did the Norfolk step dance. Most of my nine brothers and sisters played a musical instrument and that's how we entertained ourselves. I was always on the accordion. The Newstead family made up the Cockthorpe Band in the 1930s and we entertained in the villages around. We started again properly after the war, although we did some entertaining in the pubs during the war.

Walter Newstead (COCKTHORPE)

*M*y earliest memories concern the concert parties in the church hall. Kate Reeve was very good at recitations while Bert Leverett excelled with his rendition of "When Father Papered the Parlour". We all had to say our piece. Later came dances in the hall and I remember Jack Thrower and Ernie Algar playing accordions with Charles Stewart on piano and Sidney Talbot on drums. They had to disband when war broke out.

Doris Beeby (SCOLE)

*A*s a lad of five or six I remember waiting for the big hitters Harry Hewitt and Blondin Wilkins to smash the ball out of the ground. Russell Bryant and I learned to play the game between two barns on a concrete pathway using a draining rod for a bat and a golf ball. I remember the concrete wicket and coconut matting which had to be put out every weekend while the cows were removed an hour or so before play. Most of the people in the village would travel with the team on the bus to what seemed faraway places in those days - Cley, Blakeney, Bodham, Thornage, Sheringham and Aldborough.

David Briggs (BRADFIELD)

A smart musical set at Burnham Market

I remember peace celebrations after the First World War in Farmer Roy's barn and field. On Valentine's Day we boys were going to sing around the houses. Then they decided they didn't want me with them so I took a short cut and arrived at the tollhouse before them and received sweets. When the other boys arrived later they got nothing. The song we sang was "Good Old Mother Valentine, God bless the baker, You'll be the giver and I'll be the taker"

Sydney Watkins (GUIST)

We played all sorts of wonderful games in the playground, "Poor Mary is aweeping", "Farmer in the field", "The apples grew ripe", "Ring a Roses" etc. There was a grassy area beyond the playground where we little ones were roped into playing "Hospitals" with the bigger girls. We were the "patients" and lay on coats spread out on the grass and our "operations" were performed beneath another coat which covered both "patient" and "doctor". Thorns were used (very carefully) as "pretend" needles and red currants for pills.

Ivy West (AYLMERTON)

I suppose the greatest moment in Anmer's cricket history was the day the great Australian Keith Miller came with an RAF team. He made a quick 50 and broke his bat in the process. My proudest moment was batting against the formidable Arthur Mailey a few years after the war. He was over here as cricket correspondent for an Australian paper and staying with Col. Hancock at Grimston. Col. Hancock always brought a team over to play us on the August Bank Holiday Monday.

Robert Hooks (ANMER)

*B*ack in the early 1960s we used to play darts at Fersfield Magpie when there were ten players in a team. And the Fersfield team always read: Hoskins and Hoskins; Hoskins and Hoskins; Hoskins and Hoskins; Hoskins and Hoskins; Tom Shillings and Frank Kitchen. Oh, and a Hoskins kept the pub.

Neville Day (HEMPNALL)

Hempnall School football team of 1948-49. Back row (left to right): Bill Moore, Robin Moore, Maurice Warne, Peter Emms, Hilton Smith, Eddy Sauvereign; Front row: Ray Youngman, Billy Youngman, Neville Day, Basil Warne, Bernard Youngs, Dave Etheridge

Last Orders, Please!

Pubs, like village characters, simply aren't what they used to be and trying to work out how many rural hostelries have closed in the past three or four decades will drive you to drink! A little summary soaked in cynicism, although the changing role of the village pub does reflect many of the ways the communities around it have altered. Pubs have been forced to diversify, and some are more like restaurants in the same way a lot of garages resemble supermarkets.

Passing trade and people popping out for a meal have taken over from a hard core of regulars pubs used to depend on for survival. There are places where the description "local" is a total misnomer.

The growth of the holiday trade has kept certain inns afloat, although it is hard to detect much of a true community atmosphere in the bar. Pool tables, satellite television, fruit machines, Karaoke and chicken in a basket may be the acceptable trappings of the tripper. But they do nothing to lure back the older locals who remember pubs putting the emphasis on a homely welcome and a familiar face.

Giant combines have mowed down most of the small breweries, while the old-fashioned landlord or landlady, poised with a greeting and a pint of your usual, have been ousted by quick-serving, fast-talking tenants who want to know if that will be all, Sir?

The idea of dropping into the local for a laugh and a chat is largely regarded as no more than a sentimental leftover from an age when people didn't leave the village except for National Service, a Norwich City Cup run or the Royal Norfolk Show.

However, these progressives tend to forget how many villages had more than one watering hole ... so you could support more than one brewery and tell the same story at least twice a week.

The Ratcatchers used to be a guest house and when it first applied for a licence in 1901 the local vermin exterminator was staying there while working in the area. So they named it after him. Thank goodness he wasn't a honeycart driver!

Jill Charlier (CAWSTON)

There was a pub in the village called the Norfolk Hero. During the Second World War the landlord was Jimmy Brown, a likeable character noted for selling his beer by the pailful. When beer was rationed Jimmy always had a plentiful supply. There were a few locals but the pub was usually packed out with airmen from RAF Bircham Newton and soldiers from nearby searchlight posts. A pail of beer would be placed in the middle of the bar floor. As the mugs emptied they would be dipped into the pail for a refill - not very hygienic but, as far as I know, no-one ever died from it.

Ted Beales (STANHOE)

On Saturday evenings in the garden of the Lion Inn they used to stage quoit matches. My father won one of these and the prize was an oak and silver biscuit barrel which I still have in my possession.

Victoria Page (THURNE)

It's a Morgan's house - Scottgate Inn at Terrington St. John, near King's Lynn

*I*n 1948 when I was six I moved to Norfolk from London. My father, born at Gimingham, was happy to be back in his home county. My parents took the licence of the King's Head, now known as the Ark. I remember being allowed in the bar on a Sunday evening to step dance. George Craske came from Tunstead and played the accordion. The children in the village laughed at my cockney accent ... so every night I would lie in bed and practice to speak the Norfolk tongue.

Marion Daniels (ERPINGHAM)

Trunch Brewery workers ready to roll out the barrels in the 1920s!

I was nursing at the Norfolk & Norwich Hospital in 1942. My home was at Reepham and I used to cycle back sometimes on my half-day off. One evening I was on my way to Norwich and had to be in by 10pm. The sky was alive with planes. Norwich was being bombed again. Suddenly there was a torrential shower of rain and so I made a beeline for the Bell and sheltered in the porch. I dare not go in as I hadn't enough money on me for a drink. But someone spotted me, opened the door and welcomed me in to the cosy, dry little bar. It was like a little bit of heaven for a weary, wet and worried junior nurse.

Ann Dickinson (ALDERFORD)

J took over at the Eagle Tavern in 1969, and we were well supported by the local community and Broads holidaymakers. We won the Blakes Pub of the Year Award three years running and, of course, we had our characters like Eric Clitheroe, an ex-paratrooper who was able to reverse his feet so that it appeared his body was facing in the opposite direction. To see him walking up a ladder was something to behold. We had our own ghost, a gambler and a very successful one. Several times in the dead of night we heard the jackpot being paid out on the fruit machine. On investigation we found all the money in the tray and this with the machine being unplugged from the electricity supply. We called in the experts, Bell Fruit of Norwich, who assured us that such a thing was totally impossible. But it did happen .... Sadly the Eagle is no more. The brewery closed it several years ago and so another little bit of Norfolk disappeared for ever.

Norman Wakeham (NEATISHEAD)

T here were five public houses in Old Buckenham and this is how we remembered them ... The Sun shall shine on the Prince of Wales, who will wear a Crown, ride a White Horse and be a Jolly Sportsman. (The Ox and Plough was previously the Crown).

Kathleen Bertvick (OLD BUCKENHAM)

Plenty of shade outside the Black Horse at Castle Rising near King's Lynn

Mine host waits for his customers, with Bullard's Beers to the fore

*M*y grandfather, Robert Killengrey, was licensee of the White Horse for 59 years. I always wonder if this is a record. When he took over the pub it was a Morse & Woods of Swaffham house. It later became a Steward & Pattesons pub. A gentleman called Mr. Lunn used to call every month for the money. My husband, William held the White Horse licence for 26 years, but in 1977 the brewery decided to close it. In fact, October 6th, 1977 proved to be a very sad day. I was leaving a house I had lived in for 57 years and with which a Killengrey had been associated for 85 years. The pub was refurbished and reopened.

Elsie Palmer (LONGHAM)

*T*he Union Tavern public house was next door and well I knew it on a summer's evening when my bedroom window was open and I couldn't get to sleep because of all the merriment at closing time! My father, John McWhinney, commonly known to everyone as Mac, used to give the landlord a lift with the barrels of beer. We always knew what was meant when we heard a call at the back gate. "Ready when you are, Mac!". Father always went at the double. How many pints he got out of it we never really knew.

Mary Holmes (SMALLBURGH)

I remember the fire at the old Three Boars pub, which was on the first Sunday in May 1926. Of course the fire engine was drawn by horses.

Mary Godfrey (SPOONER ROW)

*A*s a child I would listen to Granfar Palmer playing his concertina at the Friday dance. On this occasion there was a large crowd present which was rather lucky for one young lady wearing violet-coloured French knickers. The elastic snapped as she was dancing and as they fell to her ankles she carefully moved her partner through the crowd and into a corner where she kicked them under a chair. They were found the next day and hung over the fireplace in the Red Lion for many a long year.

Alec Hunt (HOLME HALE)

*M*y husband and I took over as licensees of the Horseshoes in 1971 and stayed for a dozen years. About two years after we got there it was discovered that Jimmy Crane, Tom Fox and Herbert Witham had all been drinking in the pub for 60 years. Herbert lived to celebrate another ten years of drinking at the Shoes. During our time an annual harvest festival and auction was started in the pub, the money raised going to local charities.

Marian Daniels (ALBY)

Adventures in the meadows

Mention Necton and I am immediately transported back to Whalebone Farm in the late 1950s. I made weekend and holiday visits to Grandad Lemmon's farm. It was only a small 30-acre farm with a few animals and a couple of arable fields, probably a modern farmer's nightmare! What adventures were to be had in those meadows, not the sterile pastures of today but small green havens surrounded by thick hedges, dotted with trees and wild flowers. To a boy a pond became the sea, a wet cart track a river and a haystack a castle.

John Missing (NECTON)

Dewin' Diffrunt

Every village, it seems, was a stage for the real characters of rural life, the majority endearing themselves to more orthodox members of a small society by dint of eccentric mannerisms or dress.

It was easy to stand out in a little crowd, and I am fairly certain that some of the folk to make a memorable mark ended up doing or saying things simply because it was expected of them.

Humour could be rustic, repetitive and sometimes a little rough and ready, but it was an integral part of country life especially when the yarns flowed along with the ale at the pub. There were always natural targets for aggravation.

Of course, some communities absorbed more unusual personalities than others, although many people who spent their formative years in a Norfolk village will claim they lived through the golden age of the character.

That is as contentious as suggesting life was more fun in the 1930s or 1940s than it is today, but it does serve to underline a lasting affection, and occasionally respect, for the folk who refused to conform to "normal" standards.

Reflections here also include personalities whose service beyond the call of duty earned them elevation to the "character" elite - people like Granny Stiles, who delivered babies, tended the sick and laid out the departed, and Amy Gricks, who played the organ at both Hockering and Mattishall Burgh churches for 50 years.

Jimmy Moody was one of the few local people to own a car. It was a very ancient vehicle and on approaching a corner or road junction he would get out and look round to see all was clear before proceeding. Another character who sticks out was part-time scrap merchant Charlie Hendry. At one time I was most anxious to buy from him a second-hand three-speed cycle hub. The one and sixpence he wanted for it always seemed just out of reach. When my savings reached one and tuppence ha'penny I had the brilliant idea that if I took this to him all in ha'pennies, I could collect the hub, hand over the money and do a bunk before he could count it. I did this out of desperation and I can still hear the shouts ringing in my ears as I disappeared from his yard; "Come back, you young varmint!"

Malcolm Howell (BURNHAM MARKET)

George Bailey and Prince, outstanding characters from Rickenhall take a stroll through the village in the early 1960s. They had just been drilling sugar beet with a drill 100 years old. Prince appeared in a film, "Village in the Wheatfield", made in Rickenhall and shown all over the county

We kept a cow and supplied milk to Lucy Grey, an old lady with failing sight who lived alone in a clay cottage just up the road from us but on the opposite side. Every afternoon she came with her enamel can. Crossing the road was always hazardous as her hearing was also unreliable. We lost count of the number of times she was knocked down and carted off to hospital at death's door only to reappear as usual a few days later. Next door to her lived Ted Sheldrake, known as Buttonhole Joe. He was a familiar sight with his large red nose, white walrus moustache and his trademark, a buttonhole, usually a rose and always plucked from his colourful cottage garden. He had worked on the railway and helped build the swing bridge at Reedham. He never went anywhere without his bowler hat and walking stick.

Anne Battley (FLORDON)

S ilfield Street leads to the main road between Wymondham and Ashwellthorpe. This corner was a meeting place for men and boys of the village in the late 1930s and was known as the News Corner. Some names spring immediately to mind ... my Uncle Fred Hireson, Long Will Quantrell, Walter Barber's father with his clay pipe and leather boots with the laces always undone, and Harry Browne whose wife was headteacher at the village school.

Reg White (SILFIELD)

M y Uncle Gilbert was a most interesting man. He arrived in Norfolk from the West Country as an officer in the Church Army. He travelled round the villages in a horse-drawn caravan holding mission meetings at every stop. Having been attracted to my aunt he set up home in Stibbard where he started in business selling and recharging accumulators which were used to run early non-mains radios in 1929.

Jim Baldwin (STIBBARD)

Basket-making skills were handed down by Litcham's Ben Howard (left) to his son Arthur, who was also the village postman and chairman of Litcham Oddfellows

I lived in Marshland Street and the sweep lived opposite. Horace Reeve used a donkey to carry his brushes and bags of soot. The donkey slept in the house with him and his wife. We also had our very own weatherman. Cecil Tibbet lived with a houseful of cats. He used to ride a moped with a box of chestnuts on it and a large notice saying; "Stop me and buy some". We had a cobbler, Mick Sayers, and his was the sort of shop you went into not just to get your shoes mended but to appreciate the warm welcome. The seats were always full of folk having a natter.

Jean Bartrum (TERRINGTON ST CLEMENT)

*J*ohn Bore lost a leg in the Great War, but he had his own little market garden which he cultivated entirely by himself. He had a cart rather like a hen house on wheels. This was drawn by Toby his donkey and he used to sell vegetables round Wiveton and Cley. When delivering his produce to the George Hotel at Cley he would be joined by the hotel dog also called Toby and the dog would accompany him on the rest of the round. As they passed Miss Starr's shop John Bore would wrap some money in his handkerchief and give it to the dog. Toby the dog would go to the shop and return with a bar of chocolate for all three to share.

Margaret Loose (WIVETON)

*M*y Great Uncle, Richard Thomas, loved children although he was never married. He owned one of the first cars in the village and, of course, all the youngsters wanted a ride. He would tell them; "Nobody rides in my car without paying." So he would line them all up and give them a penny each. Then he charged them a penny for a ride round the village. He also played the church organ but could not read music. If he started a hymn in the wrong key he'd stop and shout; "Whoa, whoa ... Let's have another go!" until he got the right key.

Eleanor Small (ROUGHAM)

*T*apper Margerson, the local shepherd, used to do the village football tote. He would call round for my father to draw the teams out of his bag. Very often when he stuck his hand in the bag he would pull out a dead mole. Tapper died several years ago but the Scout and Cub hut built in Pigsty Lane is named after him as it was built on his land. Denys Rokeby was the Vicar who always wore a big black hat and a long black coat. If you met him he would raise his hat and ask why you were not in church on Sunday.

Janet Bailey (MUNDFORD)

Jimmy Tilney was a real old character. I remember when a good friend of mine, Mrs. Woodhouse, had a load of logs delivered. They were put over a wall on to her lawn. After dark Jimmy brought his barrow over and helped himself to some. He took them back to his place, chopped up the logs and next day went and sold her some for kindling. Jimmy's little ditty was "You can't judge the marmalade by the label on the jar." He used to sing that in the Bull after a pint.

Mary Taggert (LITCHAM)

I shall always remember Ted Constable, church verger and gravedigger. A serious person, he always looked as if he ate young lads for breakfast. He wore flared bottom trousers with buttons on the sides. In church he used to say the "Amens" about two seconds after the rest of us. Billy Drew was a roadman who watched the world go by. He would occasionally lean on his broom, the end of the handle in his hands under his chin. It was claimed that a local lady stopped in her pony and trap one day to point out the dangers of a handle going into his throat. He never broke the habit, bless him!

Robbie Head (EAST LEXHAM)

One character who will not be forgotten is Martha Cullum, Aunt Martha to all of Bawburgh. In pre-National Health days she was the local "wise woman" to whom people turned in trouble. She delivered babies, laid out the dead, sat up at nights nursing the sick and was even known to push a patient she was worried about all the way to the doctor at Costessey in a bath chair.

Cynthia Thompson (BAWBURGH)

We used to go to Blakeney every year for the Regatta. What fun - the greasy pole, the sailing, the fair, collecting cockles and bringing them home to cook for tea. But the first person we always had to visit was Jacob Holliday in his little cobblers shop. I used to be in awe of him because his long white beard made me think of pictures of Jesus. On Sundays he went to chapel dressed all in black with a black hat on his head. He would never talk to us on Sundays.

Dora Brown (BLAKENEY)

Umbrella Joe collected the name because he always carried an umbrella and would give you a weather forecast when you met. I remember pushing a neighbour's baby out with my brother and we met Joe for the first time. I was so scared I left the pram and ran the two miles home as if the devil was behind me, leaving my brother to bring the baby back.

Mary Lambert (BESTHORPE)

Donkey cart transport at Hethersett for the old-style sweep, "Dusty" Goodings, all the way from Wymondham

J'll never forget Canon Bracecamp, widely known as the Tramp Parson because of the time he spent with tramps and down-and- outs while preparing for his ministry. He was a legend in his lifetime. His magnetic personality, dynamic energy, vision and loving care for all the people of Ormesby irrespective of class or creed, rich or poor, uplifted, transformed and inspired all around him. As one who practised what he preached, he had a welcome in every home and every heart. He is buried in Ormesby.

Jim Holmes (ORMESBY)

*H*arry Middleton, known to most as Old Cye, was respected by young and old alike. He could be seen until shortly before his death sitting on a seat near his home sporting a flower in his buttonhole. The larger the flower, the better Cye liked it. I have seen him wearing a dahlia as big as a tea plate, He lived in a silent world for over 60 years, being deaf since he was kicked in the head by a horse while at work as a young man at Thornham. He was a dog lover and until a short time before he died he had one to keep him company. The last three were named Moonlight, Starlight and Daylight.

Ted Beales (DOCKING)

The earliest resident of Barton Hall, Michael Trubshawe, latterly a bit-part film actor with roles in The Titfield Thunderbolt and another film depicting the relief of Brussels in World War Two, was responsible for the formation of the Norfolk Bitterns Cricket Club, now sadly defunct. Trubby was a useful cricketer and a real character. His speciality was a ritual. Every time he lost his wicket, usually by being caught, he would walk back to the pavilion and when about five or ten yards away hurl his bat into the wood, yelling for all to hear; "I shouldn't have hit the bloody thing!"

Peter Neave (BARTON TURF)

Gamekeeper, dog, gun and rabbit - such a familiar Norfolk scene

We had three bells rung at our wedding by George Mullenger. He had one rope on his foot and rang the other two with his hands ... a one man bellringing team!

Dorothy Cason (SHIMPLING)

My grandmother, Blanche Styles, delivered the new babies, looked after the sick and laid out the dead in Winfarthing and surrounding villages. This was before district nurses, funeral directors and funeral parlours as we know them today. The nearest doctor was in Diss and in any event people had to pay to see him. Granny Styles was my grandmother but she was known as Granny Styles to all and sundry.

Elizabeth Pyle (WINFARTHING)

Amy Gricks used to play the organ at both Hockering Church and St Peter's, Mattishall Burgh. She did this for 50 years. Amy had a bicycle but didn't ride it in the dark. The winter used to see her, along with husband for company, walking the roads for miles at a time. She was a very devoted servant.

Mary Gricks (HOCKERING)

Miss Dick Whittleton was my Great Aunt, who was, in fact, christened Violet. She hated the name and would much have preferred to be a boy. So as a child she decided to be called Dick. The name stuck and she was always known by it and that is why she appears in Kelly's Directory of Norfolk for 1900 as Whittleton, Dick (Miss), grocer.

Mary Trett (HAPPISBURGH)

Uphill all the way

Quarles, this little place not far from Wells, is one of the loveliest spots to live in. I fell in love with it 64 years ago when my father moved here as second team-man for Mr. William Hudson. We were cyclists at Quarles in those days and so knew it was always uphill to the village. It is high above sea level and from the old church ruin you can see the sea between Wells and Stiffkey by day, and if it is clear the lights of Boston across the Wash at night. Coke of Norfolk's daughter lived here for a time last century and she called it "Squalls".

Ben Taylor (QUARLES)

Church and Chapel

There may have been mixed feelings about having to learn a recitation - but there was no doubting the attractions of the reward!

A recurring theme of letters about church and chapel was the Sunday School Anniversary, an event which drew one of the biggest village gatherings of the year. A visiting preacher would introduce the items, rendered with varying degrees of confidence by youngsters often wearing brand new clothes for the occasion.

Those who regarded the whole affair as a rehearsal for purgatory had to find consolation in treats that followed - sports, picnics and trips to the seaside. There were unconfirmed reports in one parish of some crafty children wheedling their way on to both church and chapel outings ... all in the proper ecumenical spirit, of course.

The chapel, claiming close links with the agricultural workers' union movement, often boasted larger regular attendances than the parish church. Perhaps the extra attraction here was the variety offered by travelling Methodist lay preachers, some of them truly dramatic in their pulpit performances spiced with exhortations in broad Norfolk: "Dew yew tell the Lord zackly woss the matter!" and "Git on yar knees ternite and put it ryte!" among them.

Church of England parsons certainly stayed in one place longer than is customary now, and they didn't have five or six parishes to look after. Plenty of personality points to be gained here as well, although I can't help wondering if stock generally didn't begin to fall once it became a habit to walk round the village pointing out vital repairs needed to the tower.

The begging bowl has become mighty fashionable, but even those most reluctant to contribute would accept that the village would lose something precious if it lost the church. Sadly, many little chapels have closed, although it is not uncommon to see one converted into an attractive village home.

The church has a round tower and was struck by lightning about 20 years ago. That started a small fire. The tower was repaired but the weathercock is on a bent stem as if looking skyward for rain.

Reg Hammond (Croxton, near Thetford)

*I*n the late 1930s my mother was county high jump champion for Norfolk. She was small and thin. When she was a child the Vicar was the Rev. Sidebottom. At the Rectory he had a large orchard full of fruit and as she was the smallest the other children used to throw her over a large wall to throw the fruit back. On one such day they threw her over and she landed on a tree under which sat the Vicar's large dog. She stayed in the tree for over an hour until the Vicar came to look for the dog and pulled her out of the tree. He marched her home to inform her parents. Not content with this he sat her in the front pew all alone at church on Sunday as a punishment for the entire village to see. In the middle of his sermon my mother stood up and read out a list of about 20 children who had thrown her over the wall!

Valerie Grass (WEETING)

There used to be two churches in the same churchyard at Antingham, dedicated to St. Mary and St. Margaret. They were said to have been built by two sisters, after whom they were named. St. Margaret's has long been in ruins, with just the ivy clad tower remaining

Spreading the Gospel around the villages - a regular scene in Norfolk at the turn of the century

*M*ost children went to Sunday School where we learned a "piece" to say at the Anniversary. We helped to pick flowers from Granny's garden to trim the wagon where we sat waiting our turn to perform. The Sunday School treats were held in the meadow almost opposite the chapel. We would play games and picnic on the grass.

Ivy West (GRESHAM)

*I*t was either in 1939 or 1940 that we from the Chapel Sunday School had a combined outing with the Church Sunday School - almost unheard of in those days. We walked or cycled to the station, which was about a mile from the main road, to board the special train for Cromer. It was a lovely day as we all enjoyed our tea at long tables in a very large hall. It was the first time I had ever seen a cream horn!

Barbara Smith (CLENCHWARTON)

We went regularly to the Wesleyan Reform Chapel Sunday School and I stayed on to help until I got married. The Anniversary was the highlight of my year on the second Sunday in July. We practised our hymns, recitations and dialogues for several weeks and Aunt Violet, the superintendent, had the patience of Job. On the Saturday evening we decorated the Chapel with fresh flowers from our gardens. We tied them all along the rails. To top it all we had new summer dresses for the occasion. I can remember Flo Glister making dresses for my sister and me.

Dorothy Warnes (ERPINGHAM)

My mother, Miriam Frost, was a nurse at the Isolation Hospital at North Elmham. Children at the hospital couldn't have eggs for breakfast unless their parents brought them in. My father, George Frost, superintendent of the Methodist Chapel, thought it would be a good idea if every child at the hospital could have an egg at Easter. So the congregation decorated baskets with painted eggs, and every child had a treat. The tradition continues with baskets of decorated eggs going not to the Isolation Hospital but to another worthy cause.

Margaret Fisher (NORTH ELMHAM)

Everyone connected with Rougham knew Ephraim Manning, who as well as being a great Methodist was also the county council lengthman. I can picture him now in the chapel during the singing of a well-known hymn. He would put down his book, hook his thumbs in his braces and raise the roof. One of my favourite stories concerns a missionary rally. The guest speaker had completed his sermon and announced the final hymn. He was loudly interrupted by Ephraim in broad Norfolk "Hang yew on a bit, ole partner ... we Matherdists allus hev a colleckshun and we hent had one yit!"

John Rayner (ROUGHAM)

Although we have no connection with the village, my friend and I often think of the little church there. One day back in the late 1940s we stopped to pay a visit, a hobby of ours, and just as we entered the heavens opened. And when that rain in Norfolk, well, that wholly rain! We looked round the church and as the rain continued we realised there would be no pleasure in motoring on. We found the little organ unlocked and passed the time playing and singing hymns, taking it in turn to man the pump. The rain eventually eased off and we continued on our way with grand memories of an unscheduled Songs of Praise.

Reta Stevens (TOFTREES)

The parish church stands guard over this old-fashioned scene from Trunch

The chapel was the centre of the village in those days, and the Sunday School Anniversary stood out as the big event of the year. The Chapel would be packed with extra chairs down the aisle. On hot days the door would be opened onto the A11 but then quickly closed when the recitations started because of the noise of the traffic.

Arlene Dye (BESTHORPE)

My father, J. A. Appleton, was Rector of Stibbard from 1921 until 1940. I was three months old when we moved into the Rectory and it was home for all my childhood. My father was a very practical priest and made use of drama in teaching the Faith. We did plays and pageants in church with only oil lamps, so a car headlight was propped in the vestry to beam on to the players.

Helen Cook (STIBBARD)

My father, the Rev. "Teddy" Everard, was Vicar of Ranworth from 1926 until 1971. He was often dubbed the Bishop of the Broads and Ranworth Church was known as the Cathedral of the Broads. He was also responsible for starting the annual service at St. Benet's Abbey for local people and holidaymakers. During his ministry he saw the church treated for death-watch beetle, and in August 1963 the chancel was ravaged by fire. Thankfully, the world-famous rood screen was untouched.

Simon Everard (RANWORTH)

We had a Sunday School until a few years ago, and many will remember with pleasure the Anniversaries held in the barn. A platform was erected and the place decorated with flowers. Singing in the barn was to the accompaniment of pigs grunting through the walls. I remember one boiling hot Anniversary day when the leader told the congregation that he would love to take his jacket off but he thought he had better not as he was wearing his working braces.

Elsie Race (LIMPENHOE)

My father, Bernard Ritson, was Rector of Winfarthing from 1947 until his death in 1961. He never did learn to drive and was a familiar figure cycling round the village on his "sit-up and beg" black bicycle. Good Friday was always special. After the three-hour church service my mother would organise a team of volunteers to go primrosing. We all turned up with baskets of various shapes and sizes and scoured the ditches and hedgerows. The gorgeously sweet-scented flowers were used to decorate the church for Easter Sunday.

Faith Codd (WINFARTHING)

Happy band of pilgrims from Burham Market to Wells! The Gospel Hall members on their outing to the beach in the 1930s

J have happy memories of conducting Sunday School Anniversaries at Beachamwell. A Mr. Brunton was superintendent and he also played the organ. As he was very deaf he was unable to hear when I announced the hymn. I used to give him the down by raising my hand and then he would start to play. I recall when an afternoon service was about to start two little girls came in all dolled up with their Anniversary dresses on. One had a pink hat and the other a blue one. I asked myself where I had seen hats like that before. Then it dawned on me … they were "Kiss Me Quick" hats from Yarmouth with the words taken off!

Jack Gaskin (BEACHAMWELL)

C hoir boys and girls who attended the church eight o'clock service on festival days were rewarded with a threepenny piece and a bun. Our Sunday School treat was usually on St. Swithin's day at the Rectory with games and a tea.

Bernard Dennis (BINTRY)

Everything You Need!

"Talking shop" used to mean catching up with all the local news while you bought a bar of soap, a reel of cotton, a quarter of tea and a tin of condensed milk.

Most villages had a store able to provide the essentials of life. Some boasted with every justification that they had "everything you need" - and they delivered as well. Stammers of Hempnall, which opened in 1840, covered an area of about 10 square miles, switching from a horse and cart to motor transport in 1925.

The delivery man served 40 villages and customers were always pleased to see a regular visitor. They rarely saw anyone else other than the man who brought the groceries. Few items were pre-packed in those days; sugar, tea, soda and pepper arrived at the shop in large quantities and had to be weighed and bagged.

Dramatic changes in shopping patterns, many of them prompted by the age of the car, have left too many villages without a store. Where they remain, ever-increasing overheads and the inducements of the nearest supermarket make it a desperate fight for survival.

Bad weather, of course, can be a blessing for the local shop as villagers "rediscover" it while roads are blocked - but this new-found loyalty usually melts along with the snow.

In remote areas of Norfolk, where public transport is non-existent, the shop and post office are vital facilities for the elderly as they collect their pensions and provisions. The question is how much longer they can hang on...

We moved here from London, and one of my favourite memories will always be the shop run by Allan Jarvis. It was open until 8 o'clock at night. It had the mandatory chair for the customers, the hand-used bacon slicer and there were those beautiful polished drawers on the wall complete with a large clock over the back room doorway. Going into the shop was like entering a time capsule. Mind you, you got a lot of things there that you cannot get today - politeness, helpfulness and the feeling that all the staff actually had time for you.

Sylvia Rotchell (TERRINGTON ST CLEMENT)

There was a shop in a row of eight very small houses where a lady sold sweets, cigarettes and tobacco. You could buy a farthing's worth of sweets and that meant quite a few. The lady next door kept the village post office and the mail used to be collected around 3 am. A pole was passed through a hole underneath the bedroom windowsill. The mailbag was placed on the end of the pole and dropped into the mail cart.

Miriam Morris (CROXTON, NEAR THETFORD)

My grandfather, Ernest Wheals, used to drive to Norwich in his pony and trap to buy tea at Eddington's, leaving his transport outside the shop on the Walk. When he died in 1914 the post office and shop were carried on by his widow and subsequently by my parents, not passing out of the family until 1958. The other post office in Saham Hills was also with the same family, the Carters, from about 1918.

Pat Newton (SAHAM TONEY)

Meat delivered by horse and cart. F. Archer of Wendling, near Dereham, had a pipe-smoking chap at the reins

My father, John William Clingo returned to his home village in 1921 and started a bakery business. It was horse and cart in those early days. In the early 1930s he bought a nearly new Morris Minor van for £100. Three times a week I had to deliver bread to a farmhouse down a dirt track. In the summer I could bike with a basket attached, but in winter I had to walk carrying the bread in a sack on my back. Sometimes before it got too "slubby" I would be a bit adventurous and take the bike. More than once I landed up in the dyke, bike, bread and all.

Mabel Nixon (SOUTHERY)

My parents Billy and Emily Horner kept the village shop in King Street from about 1933. The shop was an institution, a meeting place for most local people. Whole cheeses were sliced to suit and slab fruit cake cut to requirements. There was a chemistry cupboard for aches and pains, glass jars full of sweets, a bank of small drawers containing untold little items like pins and needles and there was even hardware and hoes for the sugar beet, bicycle tyres and tubes, twinsets, socks, underwear, Corona and paraffin. The shop used to be open from 9 am to 8 pm during the week and from 9am to 9pm on Saturdays. Saturday afternoon and evening made up "Grocery Day". Father also had a smallholding just up the road from the shop with pigs, chickens and bullocks. We also had a Jersey cow for our own milk.

John Horner (NEATISHEAD)

My uncle, Ralph Wells, spent 50 years delivering bread for the local baker. He was the first to try out a motor van bought by the firm but he was still delivering with his horse, Jolly, when he retired in 1962. He said: "There's one thing about a horse, it will always start, whereas a van won't." He claimed his horse knew every stop on the round by heart. "He would not let me go past one" said Ralph. He was not the only tradesman in the village to use that mode of transport. When he retired the milkman and coalman still used a horse and cart.

David Moore (COLTISHALL)

I was born opposite the main village shop and post office kept by Mr. Freddie Brown. It was a real delight to go in with all the large tins of biscuits to choose from and everything cut and weighed out while you sat on a high chair beside the counter. At Christmas the top store room was turned into a fairyland of toys, books and games. There was a smaller shop just up the street. We had three bakers, two butchers shops and two butchers who came twice a week by horse and cart. Hannah Piggot came round once a week with fish, again delivering by horse and cart.

Hazel Kay (BLAKENEY)

Welborne Post Office and Stores, near East Dereham just before the First World War. Mr. Heyhoe the postman collects the letters

During my early years I remember bread being delivered by horse and cart by Mr. Clements from Flitcham. Mr. Raspberry from Gayton and Mr. Twite from Grimston would bring round the green groceries, and meat was also delivered by horse and cart by Mr. Elsegood from Pott Row.

George Smith (CONGHAM)

Friday night was a highlight night when the mobile fish-and-chip van called. The cooking was done inside the van using coal as fuel. Smoke used to pour out of the chimney and the smell of the smoke and cooking always arrived before the van. Ice-cream tricycles with insulated boxes over the two front wheels used to visit the village regularly. A bus called on Fridays to take passengers to Diss market.

Pat Herbert (THELVETON)

At one time Aunt Mabel was the village shopkeeper. This meant that she kept groceries in the pantry while boxes of sweets and chocolates were sold from the top of the harmonium in one corner of the tiny living-room.

Sylvia Claxton (SHARRINGTON)

On leaving school my first job was at the stores in Helhoughton which sold everything. I worked in the drapery, sweet and post office departments. The other end of the store was for groceries and warehousing. I was married while working in the shop. My husband was doing his National Service and was sent to the Suez Canal. I continued to work in the shop for 18 months until he came home.

Madge Jarvis (HELHOUGHTON)

We kept the village store for almost 40 years. Edie Pitch was working in the shop when we took over - and we left her still working there when we retired. The day we arrived at "Sunshine Stores" we found a small gentleman standing nearby, cap on head, overall, black face, sack on his back and chimney sweeping brushes peeping out of the top. We soon found out he was known to all as Brooky, and all knew him as a friend. I must also mention Mrs. Ada Loades. Every day heavily clad in long, black clothes complete with hat she would slowly walk from her house down to the shop at the same time, 10 am. She never stopped to speak. She just smiled. Her requirements were always the same. On one occasion she came round to the back door on Christmas Day wondering why the shop was closed.

Ruth Mackrell (FULMODESTON)

Fishmonger Dick Rush used to come through the village with his pony and cart shouting; "White hearin', white hearin'! far a penny, far a penny! gi'yer one in fer the bearby!" which translated is "White Herring, white herring! Four a penny, four a penny! I'll give you one extra for the baby!". His fish were delicious.

Margaret Hammond (ASHWELLTHORPE)

My dad, Amos Parker, used to deliver bread by horse and cart before going modern with a van. On Monday, Wednesday and Friday we covered the Great and Little Fransham area, while on Tuesday, Thursday and Saturday we headed for the likes of Scarning, Bradenham and Toftwood. I can remember a small loaf costing tuppence ha'penny. Flour was tenpence for three pounds. We also delivered meal for chickens which was ordered in advance and carried under or behind the seats. Dad used to work very long hours as he had to mix, knead and bake the bread before going out on deliveries. He would start at 4 am most days. I helped every Saturday as it was a long round - and we had to get home early to go to the speedway.

Audrey Newsome (WENDLING)

Plenty to attract locals and visitors alike to the Ludham Stores in Broadland in the old days

Errand boy Fred Couzens ready to deliver meat in East Rudham in 1912

Mrs. Riseborough ran a little shop from her front room selling crisps, Corona and tobacco. You knocked on the door and she brought it to you. During the war she would only let crisps go to children under 14 as they were in short supply.

Bob Thompson (BELAUGH)

I went to work at Stammers Stores, the shop that sold absolutely everything. If they didn't stock a particular item, the Governor, which is what we called Mr. G. Stammers, would soon get it. I reckon Stammers was to Hempnall what Harrods is to London. We had lovely staff outings to Yarmouth each summer which included high tea at Arnold's Restaurant and a show on the Britannia Pier.

Joy Futter (HEMPNALL)

In the Wars

Norfolk memories of the Second World War are dominated by airfields and Americans. There have been countless reunions to strengthen those international bonds forged in the 1940s.

An American pilot serving in the county said; "I guess if you just switch off and glide in you'll find you're more likely to have gotten on an airfield than any other place!"

In 1939 there were five operational airfields in Norfolk: Bircham Newton, Feltwell, Marham, Watton and West Raynham, while by the end of the war there were 37.

The "Friendly Invasion" meant a big clash of cultures, Norfolk's traditional reserve and caution set against the brashness of the Americans. There were bound to be some problems with young servicemen from the other side of the world causing the biggest upheaval many Norfolk villages had seen this century.

In the main, though, the friendly and generous nature of the Yanks won through to help create a good working relationship. Norfolk families invited them into their homes and airbases organised Christmas parties for the local children.

Many of the old airfields have long since disappeared under the plough or have been turned into industrial estates.

Evacuees from London sparking another big culture clash. Home Guard adventures and dances when the military two-step was all the rage are other items on regular parade.

An older generation recalls Zeppelins overhead and soldiers and horses marching along the village street.

My grandfather was allowed to fish on the beach which was fortified with barbed wire and steel poles, a real eyesore on the lovely beach but most necessary in case of invasion. I remember how after some ships had sunk the cargo would drift on to the shore and the locals would collect such things as oranges and even children's books. These were so soaked in salt water it was impossible to separate the pages.

Marion Read (BACTON)

West Tofts in Breckland just before the village became part of the Battle Area in the last war.

With the war came the evacuees, children from London billeted with local families to escape the bombing. We had a mother and her family with us for a while. I don't think they took to country life because they soon returned to the capital. Later on we had another evacuee from London, Ronnie Green, who soon became one of the family. Many evacuees had no experience of the countryside. Some didn't like milk from "a dirty cow" and said it ought to come from a shop. At the same time they laughed at us as we didn't know about the London Underground trains. It was a learning time for us all.

Edith Bennett (WEST TOFTS)

I can remember seeing Zeppelins almost overhead, presumably when Dereham was bombed. Our cavalry, complete with gun trailers, visited the village and wagons were parked ready for our evacuation when it was thought the Germans would invade at Weybourne. I remember that on the first day a wagon was parked outside our house in the street and the shafts were pointing towards Weybourne. Someone realised it would be better if at least we started off "inland" and the wagon was turned round in readiness!

Victor Fenn (BINTRY)

I have many memories of the Americans at Tibenham Airfield. I recall one occasion in particular when we were given a "ride" in a Liberator, and as it taxied along the runway I was crying my eyes out thinking we were leaving England and off to Germany! When we stopped we got small boxes of candy and ran home.

John Thrower (TIBENHAM)

*T*he old Jubilee Hall was destroyed by fire in about 1950. It was a wooden army type hut on the edge of Whin Common and as a lad I remember it best for the dances held there during the war years. Local bands at that time were the Melodious Aces and the Nighthawks. I can recall all the soldiers from the Searchlight Battery entrenched on Whin Common itself who always came to the dances. My mother and several other ladies from the village always managed to find very appetising refreshments despite rationing.

Gerald Mackinder (DENVER)

*W*henever I watch "Dad's Army" my mind returns to the early war years in Neatishead. My cousin, Grace Popey and her husband Billy ran the Eagle Tavern and, as a young teenager, I spent many happy weekends helping them. Their daughter Dulcie and I were out walking on a Sunday afternoon, crossing the little bridge over the stream just below the old saddler's shop run by Charlie Easton and the New Inn. To our surprise a tennis ball landed at our feet. A voice said; "You're both dead...that was a hand grenade!" Amid girlish giggles we looked to see who was under the hedge. It was Billy Horner on Home Guard duty. They were on what they called "practice manoeuvres" armed with pitchforks and tennis balls. A bit inadequate, perhaps, but the spirit was there.

Elsie Nash (NEATISHEAD)

*A*fter serving at Lakenheath and Methwold as an airframe fitter, I ended my service career at Feltwell and remember well the cinema in the main street. This was invariably packed with boisterous RAF personnel especially when Susan Hayward or Alice Faye were featured. On July 4th, 1941 a Wellington of 57th Squadron crashed at Larman's Fen a few miles from the airfield when returning from an abortive raid in Holland. Five of the six crew perished. The rear gunner survived, only to be killed five months later. An engine and complete propeller from this aircraft were recovered a few years ago and are now on display at the Fenland Aviation Museum at West Walton near Wisbech.

Peter Russell (FELTWELL)

I used to cross the airfield as a youngster accompanied by a little boy called Noel Ayton. We were, along with the other children at Oulton Elementary School, aware of the aircraft and our aeroplane recognition was quite remarkable until one day. As Noel and I were walking home from school we spotted a plane that didn't look familiar, but being young and curious we watched with fascination when, suddenly, bombs started dropping from it. Could this be target practice? Imagine our surprise when airmen yelled to us to flatten ourselves. After the explosions we dusted down and, somewhat shaken and wiser, ran home. After this a platform was erected in the infant classroom, and whenever the sirens sounded we crowded underneath and tried to carry on with our lessons. Little work was done but a great deal of fun was had. Thankfully, we didn't realise the seriousness of the situation.

Margaret Freston (Oulton, near Aylsham)

I served on destroyers in the Royal Navy during the last war and at one time was stationed in Alexandria in the Mediterranean, escorting convoys to Malta. In between convoys we used to go out at night and patrol along the North Africa coast hoping to engage enemy ships sneaking in to replenish Rommel's army. Just as dawn was breaking one morning we came across an Italian ship which we engaged and sank. We picked up a few survivors and made them strip and throw their clothes in a heap on the floor. On a blue jersey I saw a cardboard tag which read "A.B. Mackie, Sedgeford, King's Lynn, Norfolk" I put the tag in my wallet and kept it until I was demobbed in 1945. I worked for a removal firm and we were in Sedgeford to move the Vicar. This was about three months after my demob. I told him my story and showed him the tag. He borrowed it and away he went for about 30 minutes. He returned to say he had solved the mystery. I thought A.B.Mackie was an Able Seaman. It turned out she was an elderly lady knitting for the forces and she used to put a tag on everything she made.

Arthur Tuck (Sedgeford)

*O*n the first night of the war in 1939 we were awakened by Mr. Bird the air raid warden coming up the street blowing his whistle. We all put our heads out of the bedroom windows, only to be told an air raid was expected. The Home Guard was formed and my husband had to cycle to Swanton Novers for duty at the searchlight camp. We only had bikes to get us from A to B in those days and on several occasions we cycled from Barney to Banham, my husband's home, for the weekend - a round trip of 70 miles.

Mary Lanchester (Barney)

Gas masks give this line-up an eerie quality at Pickenham Hall in 1941. It was then used as an auxiliary war hospital

I can see even now the young telegraph boy in his pillbox hat handing my mother the ill-fated orange envelope, standing and waiting to take the reply. My mother did not open the envelope but said to the boy; "Thank you, there will be no answer". She seemed to know its message. It was to say that my brother, not yet 20 years of age, had been killed in action in the First World War.

Gordon Melton (DERSINGHAM)

*D*uring the war I kept a diary and on September 14th, 1942 I wrote; "There was quite a bit of excitement in the village as the contractors arrived to start on the drome". During 1943 John Laing and Sons built the airfield, consisting of a 2000-yard main runway and two intersecting runways, both 1400 yards long. Nissen huts were erected to take 2900 men. In order to clear the site some six miles of hedges were uprooted and 1400 trees felled. The drome was occupied by 452 Squadron on January 3rd, 1944 and was used for day raids with Flying Fortresses marked with an 'L' on the tail. Over 100 planes were lost on operations.

Violet Jeffery (DEOPHAM)

I was fortunate enough to be evacuated there with my mother and another lady and her two children. We were all taken to Holly Farm and given half of the farmhouse to live in. Could children from the outskirts of London possibly be more lucky! Mr. and Mrs. Russell, or Russ and Auntie Annie as we called them, and their son Oliver made us so very welcome.

Christine Roe (INGHAM)

I recall my dad opening our back door during the blackout and causing a German plane to drop six bombs in a line from Kempstone to Beeston. I used to stand and count the American planes leaving and returning and see all the ladies painted on the sides.

Gillian Moulton (GREAT DUNHAM)

I remember as a child of three in 1916 when a whole regiment of horse and foot soldiers marched through our village. I can still see that long line of soldiers reaching for over a mile marching with arms swinging and brass badges shining from their caps, and I still see the hundreds of horses and mules pulling the limbers and the band playing.

Sidney Talbot (THELVETON)

I think it was in October 1942 that we noticed a parachutist descending in the direction of the sugar beet field at the back of our house. Dad ran to meet him as he landed and brought him home. He appeared to be limping and I thought he was injured. But in fact he was wearing only one boot. The other had landed at Mundesley. He was very concerned about the rest of the crew; in fact the pilot had managed to land the Liberator in a field at Southrepps. Unfortunately the parachute of one young airman had failed to open and he had plunged to his death at Suffield. The pilot later came with others to collect the airman. He left his parachute of pure silk for me to have made into a wedding dress when I grew up. Two days later military police called for it!

Grace Briggs (BRADFIELD)

I was working on the farm at about seven years old in 1944. I was using the horse rake near the hangar and could hardly pull the tines up and push my foot down at the same time to release the straw. Some Americans sitting on the fence asked if they could have a go. I said no because I didn't want to get into trouble with the farmer, Billy Butcher. But they offered me candy and gum and I let them finish the field off for me. Billy thought I'd done ever so well.

John Gilbert (WENDLING)

Farriers and grooms of the Norfolk Yeomanry at Melton Constable in 1914

I was a member of a little dance band we ran in the village called the Rhythm Boys. We ran dances on Monday and Friday nights and on several occasions played on as we heard bombs and land mines being dropped in the surrounding area. The first night the Americans from Shipdham airfield descended on us in 1942 the hall was full to bursting. The caretaker, Billy Cordy, who acted as doorman on dance nights, had a tin full of dollars. We'd never seen anything like that before. There were regular fights, but none of our little band ever got involved. We tried to keep playing, hoping the fighting would give way to dancing.

Victor Cook (HINGHAM)

I saw bombs falling on the Rectory during the last war. It was a Saturday morning in 1941 and I stood in the field as a plane came over and dropped five bombs. Part of the Rectory was demolished. I was concerned because my father was lighting the church boiler ready for the Sunday services. Thank God the bombs were not released a split second sooner; otherwise there would have been no church, no school and no father!

Norman Cooper (BACONSTHORPE)

Etched in the Memory

The floods of 1912. The snowdrifts of 1947. The Coronation of 1953 (when it rained). The Big Blow of October 1987.

Certain dates beyond family anniversaries stand out as we mull over the years, and there are plenty prepared to admit they can remember clearly something that happened half a century ago, but they have real problems recalling an event from last week!

Big celebrations like Royal Weddings and the 50th anniversary of VE Day still herald street parties and teas in the village hall. Local carnivals and garden fetes still provide plenty of footage for newspapers and home recording equipment. We are still creatures of habit looking for milestones to mark and more memories for the scrapbook.

Childhood days in the village before instant entertainment and easy access to the nearest town gave anticipation a keener edge. The May Fair on the green inspired stories that had to be kept in circulation until that time came round again. The day the place went on the mains. The first car in the village (and how often that belonged to the doctor). The opening of the new village hall. The time a television crew came to do a feature on country life. The party to celebrate Grannie Pinkerton's 100th birthday. All part of the memory game, and access to full and accurate details can settle so many arguments.

Every village ought to have a chronicler, either with a pencil and notebook or a computer, to make sure important dates and events are duly observed and preserved for future generations. The regular flow of beginnings and ends may seem inconsequential at the time but they make up local history.

The furthest my granny ever travelled was to Yarmouth on the wherry when my father was a baby. I was told he cried all the way there and back until they gave him some bread and milk. Gran also went to the theatre in Norwich and remembered the one play she ever saw for the rest of her days. Thirty two years ago, when my daughter was born, my father took her by taxi to Yarmouth to see how it had changed. She went into a toyshop for the first time and bought her new great granddaughter a cuddly toy.

Avril Smithson (BRAMPTON)

*H*ighlight of the year was the May Fair. There was a large cattle sale with most of these driven along the roads from surrounding villages. The school being on the village green meant it was not safe for children to be around with the sale ground so near, so a day's holiday was granted. There was also a funfair which took up a good part of the green and ran for three nights.

Anne Williamson (BRISTON)

*E*lectric light came to Wortwell in 1932 and I still recall the excitement when it was due to be switched on. The installation allowed was three lights and one plug and each quarter we were allowed 20 units of electricity free.

Malcolm Dove (WORTWELL)

*R*oughton had a distinguished visitor in 1933. Professor Albert Einstein was sacked from his post as Director of the Kaiser Wilhelm Institute in Berlin because he was a Jew. He sought refuge in England and his host was Commander Locker Lampson, DSO, MP, who had a country retreat on Roughton Heath. Einstein stayed there with a "minder", Herbert Eastoe, a retired gamekeeper from the Gunton Estate, equipped with a rifle! Professor Einstein later went to America.

Betty Crouch (ROUGHTON)

Fleeing the damage at Snettisham during the 1953 floods

Memories down the line as the last passenger train leaves Burnham Market in 1952. The station was on the Heacham-Wells line. Goods trains ran until 1964

In 1930 I was the first baby to be born in the council houses which stand on the four crossways by the village hall. I remember going to Whitwell Hall for Jubilee and Coronation celebrations, complete with a firework display.

Gwen Martins (SKEYTON)

One of the main events of the year was Hospital Sunday on the first Sunday in July with representatives of the Hospital Association, the Methodists, Church of England and Salvation Army speaking from a farm wagon. Tea was served to the officials and the band in the WI hut. Trays of cakes appeared on the Saturday from Terry Wagg's bakery at Docking but I can never remember a bill coming! I was sent round the village during the previous week to call on each house to sell hymn sheets. People bought them whether they came to the service or not. I still remember the person who put in half a crown and asked for change. I was pleased to tell a fib and say I couldn't get the base off the collecting box.

Beryl George (STANHOE)

*C*olonel Barnham and his family gave a big party in the barn to celebrate the Coronation in 1937. I have a New Testament given me on that day and we also received a mug and a shilling. It was my birthday that day, a special event I shared with Barbara Howlett. I guess that was the biggest birthday party we ever had!

Peggy Brown (GRISTON)

I wonder if anyone remembers the day Edgar Sparrow's blacksmith's shop and house on the Green caught fire? It had a thatched roof and was soon blazing merrily. When it was well alight the New Buckenham Fire Brigade, pulled by the same horses they used for funerals, came slowly clip-clopping over the Green - all too late, of course! We children watched it all from the school window.

Pat Freeman (OLD BUCKENHAM)

*H*ighlight of the year came on June 21st and 22nd when the fair came to Aldborough Green. People used to walk for miles for the event, but we were not allowed out the first day as they used to do what they called "dickey dealing" and the horses would tear up and down the road before being bought or sold.

Sylvia Waters (ALDBOROUGH)

I spent my childhood and working life in Oxborough and was in charge of the gardens at Oxburgh Hall for more than 30 years, first with Sir Edmund Bedingfield and later with the National Trust. I can clearly remember a night in October 1917, when a German Zeppelin dropped 11 bombs in fields around the village, one within 150 yards, breaking many windows in the Hall and in the Chapel in the grounds.

Fred Greef (OXBOROUGH)

*T*he LNER Railway had a station in our village and I can remember when we used to go shopping in King's Lynn. The fare was six old pence return. Royalty used this line to go to Wolferton. When King George V died at Sandringham, his coffin went through Wootton station on its way to London and we schoolchildren lined the platform as it went by.

Albert Ward (NORTH WOOTTON)

*D*uring the floods of 1912, before I was born, my grandfather stopped a train from disaster after the railway bridge near Tharston Mill had been washed away. For so doing he was awarded an inscribed gold watch by the Great Eastern Railway.

Margaret Salt (HAPTON)

J recall vividly an incident from the late 1950s. I was ironing costumes in readiness for our school concert that evening when there was a loud roaring noise overhead. On looking out of the kitchen window I saw a huge aeroplane coming down. At that moment my school caretaker, Barbara Riseborough, sprinted across my lawn, jumped over the hedge and began to run over the fields towards the falling plane. We got into the car and raced towards the scene of the crash. The plane was already burning and the village was suddenly alive as American cars sped down the main street. You can imagine that our concert got off to a late start as most of the lads were at the scene trying to get bits of the crashed plane.

Ivy Cafferky (FIELD DALLING)

Fun and games at Burnham Market to mark the Silver Jubilee of King George V and Queen Mary in May 1935

*M*y mother was married at Ickburgh on Boxing Day 1927, and she often told us how they had a job to get to the church because it had snowed so hard on Christmas night. It was snowdrifts all the way.

Joan Hammond (ICKBURGH)

The first winter we were married, February 1979, we were blocked in for three days. We were cut off for a similar period in 1986. Everybody shared their food stores and some travelled across fields to get milk and bread for the whole village.

Debbie King (BAGTHORPE)

My brother Albert and I were born in Kenninghall in 1916 the first set of twins to be born there for over 50 years. The Vicar's wife and the Doctor's sister (or the other way round) were our Godparents and they bought us the pram and the clothes we were christened in. We were only a few days old when father was called up for the War.

Ivy Allen (KENNINGHALL)

On being demobbed from the RAF in 1946 I came to live in Cawston in the first council houses to be built after the war. The rent was 12 shillings per week and the water rate one shilling a week.

Harold Ogden (CAWSTON)

My mother was in service as a housemaid at Haveringland Hall from 1937 until 1939. She worked for Baron and Baroness Cederstrom. The Baron was Swedish and although my mother was there for nearly three years she never once saw him. Maids were expected to keep out of sight and if they heard him coming they would scuttle away to a cupboard on the landing. Big shooting parties were held at the Hall and one of the well-known people to stay there was RAB Butler.

Pam Pearce (HAVERINGLAND)

I well remember the floods of 1947. The River Wissey broke its banks at Hilgay and the contours of the land were such that the waters all ran round to the Ferry Bank. The road there was raised up from the surrounding fen and this held the water back for a time. The village was like a huge army camp with troops filling sandbags and making a wall all along Ferry Bank. The water got so high and the pressure so much that it pushed the road up through a culvert at White Bridge. It washed a house down and the water flooded through like a breached dam. Our house overlooked the fen and it was like a sea with thousands of acres flooded.

Brian Nixon (SOUTHERY)

A Bit of Gossip

"I don't like to repeat gossip - but what else can you do with it?" A reasonable attitude in a small Norfolk village before television and tabloid newspapers provided most topics for conversation.

Storytelling was a practised art in the threshing barn, on the harvest field, down the pub, round the pump, in the shop ... anywhere with enough of an audience to make sure the presentation did not slip by unnoticed.

Tales told a hundred times before were given a new coat of paint to ensure fresh chuckles of approval. Embellishment was expected, even encouraged, to turn a homely story into a vivid rural legend. By the time they got to an adjoining parish most yarns almost defied belief!

Humorous episodes, usually edged in embarrassment for some unfortunate member of local society, were at the heart of this brand of entertainment. "Just tell us about the time ... " was the prelude to memorable Saturday night sessions at the Old Bell Inn.

Newcomers and strangers were obvious targets for gossip. Americans soon had to get used to wagging tongues during the last war but once they had found a way into a close-knit community they too enjoyed having a bit of a giggle at someone else's expense.

Perhaps the telephone has removed the communal fun such storytelling provided. Gossip can be passed on in a much more furtive manner today, while more reticent village residents wouldn't recognise a good rumour if it stopped and whispered to them in the street.

But a bit of juicy local scandal, real, imagined or even exaggerated, will always survive long enough to be repeated.

There is a legend in our family about "some land in Mundesley". It seems my grandfather, a builder in the Unthank Road area of Norwich by the name of Baron George, was one of a number of local builders and businessmen invited to Mundesley, possibly in the Edwardian building boom. They were lavishly wined and dined before being sold slices of land for building development. But after they got back to Norwich, it all fell into the sea.

Wilfrid George (MUNDESLEY)

*U*ncle Cyril and his gang of pals were well known in their teens for various pranks although, as my uncle always said, these were only harmless fun. On one occasion the manager of Lamberts shop fell out with the gang for no apparent reason and so the lads felt they really ought to do something to even the score. Very late at night they visited a barn, owned by the father of one of them, where quite a lot of sparrows were roosting. By the light of cycle lamps they gently removed the birds into a sack and carefully carried it through the village to the shop. They popped the sparrows one by one through the large letterbox. For the remainder of the night the birds had a wonderful time, picking at sacks of flour and sugar. When the poor manager opened the door next morning he was met head on by a large flock of plump sparrows. When the time came for Uncle Cyril to join up for the First World War, he told the village policeman who commented simply; "Thank God for that!" I wonder why?

Valerie Herrington (SNETTISHAM)

So what's all the news from the potting shed? Bill, Ben and Little Weed meet up at Blickling for a good old Norfolk mardle!

*M*any years ago I was travelling back to London early in the morning and decided for the first time to go via Roydon, near Diss. Slowing down to round a bend I hit some broken milk bottles and both my tyres burst. I found my way to Roydon garage to explain my plight. I left my chequebook and card in London. I had no cash on me after using it all to get petrol for the journey to see my parents. The man at the garage was absolutely wonderful. He towed me in, a distance of a mile, lent me two tyres to get back with and told me to settle next time I came down. He asked for no identification or even my address, and carried out this kind act in perfect trust.

Madge Paul (ROYDON)

*A*n outstanding boy of about ten came to live with his family in the village. His name was Bert Hazell who went on to become the MP for North Norfolk. He belonged to the Christian Endeavour Group attending the Chapel and always paid tribute to the fact that it was these meetings where he learned to speak in public.

Cecil Goodrum (SILFIELD)

I grew up in the village in the 1950s and I can remember Mrs. Clarke who kept a sweet shop in the front room of her house. She also used to put out the red flag for the doctor as he was passing through from Burnham Market to his surgery at Thornham. Patients used to put their names on a blackboard and when he saw the red flag he would stop and call on them.

Carol Vincent (TITCHWELL)

I was the last village policeman in Sporle, and I was there when they were snowed in during the late 1970s. We found the old snowplough in a dyke which hadn't been used for about 30 years. The farmer repaired it and then I commandeered a tractor to pull it. The police house was the last one on Castle Acre Road and while I was busy digging everyone else out my house froze up. I was without water and heating for several days.

Patrick Thompson (SPORLE)

*A*fter dinner each day Grandad would have forty winks. I remember doing my turn with a newspaper keeping the flies off. Once I was asked to take a pair of shoes for repair at the other end of the village. I said it was a long way to walk so Grandma told me to take the bicycle standing out front near the wall. To my utter delight on returning I was told it was mine. Grandad had been to a sale.

Pauline Bartlett (BRIDGHAM)

*A*s a youngster I recall the Royal Mail used to come through the village early in the morning. Mr. Amis, the Postmaster, used to put his walking stick out of the bedroom window and the mail van driver would hang the mailbag on the hook of the stick. The Postmaster would then haul it up for delivery later.

Maurice Williamson (INGWORTH)

*T*imes were not easy before the war and some folk had to do a bit of "lifting" to make ends meet. I remember the local bobbies laying in wait for whoever was taking carrots from a field adjoining our cottage. Dad went out in the dark to the little house down the garden. When he struck a match to light the candle he was amazed to find a man hiding in there with a sack of carrots. Dad, being an old soldier, didn't give the game away.

June Ludkin (BESTHORPE)

*D*uring strawberry time growers could load their fruit on the railway at Clenchwarton up to about 4 pm. Fruit would be transported to Manchester and Newcastle areas and sold, usually by auction early the following morning. Growers would be informed by telegram what the fruit had made and what to send the following day.

Ray Cobb (CLENCHWARTON)

I delivered papers to the Vicarage, but I never once saw a whole person. I only saw a hand which used to come round the door to take the paper in. On Fridays the same hand had money in to pay me for the week's papers.

Barbara Clark (BINHAM)

I remember this humorous incident in the village not long after the First World War. It concerned a man living on his own because his wife had left him. Either to cope with his loneliness or to continue his usual way of life, he was accustomed to spending his evenings in one or more of the three pubs then open. In due course he would return home in a happy mood. A group of local youths were aware of his circumstances and one evening when knowledge of a dead pig came to them they took charge of the corpse. On gaining entry to the man's house they dragged the dead animal upstairs and placed it in his bed. On his return the man saw a long shape tucked up in the bed and he assumed it was his wife. "Hello, my old gal!" he was heard to say. "I knew you'd fare to come back to me one day. I just knew you'd come home agin!". At that the boys listening outside must have fled, for history does not relate what happened next or how the animal's body was removed.

John Barnes (CASTON)

*M*y Uncle Ben was always getting into scrapes. The story goes that Granny, called suddenly to the back door, had left a pail of very hot water at the foot of the stairs in the front hall, ready to wash the stone flags. Ben slid down the wide, curved banisters and landed slap in the bucket of water with his legs stuck up in the air. He had a very sore bottom.

Myra Jenner (BILLINGFORD)

*T*he petrol pumps were owned by Arthur Frammingham. An American airman based at nearby Sculthorpe pulled up for petrol, leaving the engine of his big car running. Arthur duly set about filling the tank. This was a lengthy process as it was only possible to put in a half gallon at a time, cranking away and pulling a series of levers. The American obviously thought it was going to be a long job. He said to Arthur; "Guess I'd better switch her off, buddy. She's using it up faster than you're putting it in!".

Len Bridges (RINGSTEAD)

Youngsters make a pit stop at Docking in the days before the car became king

How butcher fooled the joint!

*I*t took nearly 19 years for butcher Michael Leverett to confess how he brought Docking to boiling point.

It was in September 1970 when bemused villagers called the police as the local pond began to bubble and steam as if about to erupt. A crowd soon gathered to watch the unusual spectacle.

After checking with the Rural District Council that no gas, water or electricity mains ran near the pond, the police contacted naturalist Dick Bagnall-Oakeley. He said it had been a good year for methane gas, the possible cause of this disturbance. But butcher Leverett knew different ....

When Docking was in the Village Brantub spotlight on Radio Norfolk in March, 1989, he decided to come clean. Here is his story;

"Before firms had refrigerated lorries they brought the meat packed in ice. The blocks of ice contained carbon dioxide to keep them solid. If a small piece was dropped in water it would ferment and bubble and give off a vapour like smoke.

"I put a small piece in the pond next to my butcher's shop and said to my employee we would have some fun watching the reaction of people passing by. The first woman on the scene stared in amazement. Before long there was quite a gathering, all of them making suggestions as to what it might be. One person even threw a match in to see what happened.

"We were finding this quite funny until the police were called. When it was suggested they should get a fire engine to drain the pond I really started to worry.

"I haven't told anybody the truth until today (Thursday March 16th 1989) when I rang local policeman Ted Beales. Luckily he retired in 1968."

There were no reports of irate villagers taking their revenge but butcher Leverett was extremely lucky to get away without a ducking at Docking!

Village Life Goes On . . .

For all the changes, and all the problems brought with them, an optimistic streak still asserts itself in most Norfolk villages.

Hard cores of workers openly defy suggestions that community spirit has been all but drained by the pace and complexities of life at the end of the 20th century, suggestions mainly put about by those who go to ground when there are jobs to be done.

Big projects, like building a new village hall or raising thousands of pounds to stop the church tower crumbling, can have an exciting and galvanising effect. Fears for the village school, pub or shop invariably spark lively campaigns.

Newcomers, often worldly wise, articulate and self-assured, are keen to show how to deal with threats from outside. They can set examples without putting on a blatant air of superiority.

While gaps in understanding and acceptance between the old and new populations do remain worryingly wide, many villages now accept radical changes have spelt revival. Drama societies, conservation groups, cricket clubs and Women's Institutes have either been re-formed or given every chance to flourish more.

Advances in technology and a more enlightened approach to development and public transport are among the main hopes for securing a healthy future for our villages. Commuter colonisation will continue for a while, especially around Norwich and bigger towns like King's Lynn and Yarmouth, but the prospect of more people working from home offers even the biggest settlements an opportunity to draw closer together and to leave the car in the garage for a few days at a time.

Perhaps a little of that self sufficiency underlined by proud names and their trades in Kelly's Norfolk Directory of 1900 will return to our village life as a new millenium dawns. In any event, they must survive in a spirit of independence strong enough to mean "dewin' diffrunt" is a matter of choice.

To me West Lexham is home and always will be! I have lived here for nearly 25 years from the day I was born to the present. And in all those years the village hasn't changed at all ... the same brick and flint cottages, the Saxon church of St. Nicholas and the farms. I have grown up with many of the people still living here. I live at the Old Post Office which was once the Red Lion public house. Now it is a bed and breakfast house with myself and husband, Bob, running it. Many of the guests talk about the village as if it was home to them.

Caroline Moore (WEST LEXHAM)

The village hall fund-raising committee have worked very hard over the past few years. We now have the playing field in use and funds are building up towards the village hall. Various activities have taken place. John Bolderow sat in the Green Man pub last Christmas knitting for 24 hours and raised almost £150 in sponsorship. David Moon walked from Snettisham to Cromer and raised over £400. Boys of the village did a sponsored bike ride to net over £120. A year or two ago we had a sponsored 24-hour football match on the school playing field. I think the "floodlights" were a 100w bulb on each corner post!

Dennis Firmage (LITTLE SNORING)

The Killmagrannie Pipe Band in full cry at Bodham, near Holt, as villagers enjoy a Night of Squit!

J am Seething bred and born, and I think it is a lovely village with its thatched school and church, two shops, village hall and playing field plus village pond or mere and many lovely old houses. Since 1984 I have been writing to the Americans and compiling the history of 448th Bomb Group through the men's own diaries, documents and personal recollections plus many fine photographs. They were based at Seething from 1943 to 1945 and more than 450 were killed during that time. They flew the B24 Liberator bombers. They have returned for three reunions and we have a memorial in the churchyard, books they donated to the church and to the village school. Seething airfield is still in use with a small part of the old runways used by Waveney Flying Group. On the old base are two more memorials and the restored control tower.

Pat Everson (SEETHING)

Taking a step back to raise funds for the future at Roughton, near Cromer. A Victorian Street Fair caught the imagination in the name of swelling the coffers for a new village hall

An ultra-modern look for the new village hall at Swanton Morley - ready to suit the needs of a fast-growing community.

*O*ur playgroup started in 1974. We had 27 children on the books in the old wooden pavilion. We had no hot water and in winter you had to wear a few extra jumpers. Jack Barber came to our rescue on many occasions with his blow lamp to free the water pipes. I shall never forget the morning the diggers moved in to make a start on the new centre. The children downed toys and stood by the windows for ages. They watched every brick being laid over the weeks. Here we are today in a lovely bright and warm new community centre, a thriving playgroup with 70 children and a very dedicated staff.

Judy Johnson (ROYDON NEAR DISS)

I live in what was Ickburgh school. I am sure that many people who attended it during its heyday will be interested to know that my husband and I have renovated it. If any of these folk would like to visit their old school they will be most welcome and always get a cup of tea. We are both from Aberdeen but have lived here since 1972. We thoroughly enjoy the peace and quiet and the wildlife around us in Breckland. I do miss the hills, though!

Liz Cowe (ICKBURGH)

We have only lived in this village for about four years but they have been happy ones. There are several new houses which means outsiders have come here, but we have all been made welcome. There is no pub, no post office, no shop and no local bus service. But there is a Heritage Society and their fund-raising has helped keep the church in good repair. They have also presented a very nice sign to the village. The church is our meeting place and the women made a very attractive village quilt showing 20 of the village buildings. This proved an ideal way of getting to know each other. We had a good natter as we were sewing.

June Rumsby (TUTTINGTON)

I came to Worstead to take over the New Inn pub with my husband Mike and son Daniel from Liverpool over four years ago. You can imagine how scared we felt coming to a small village from the city. We needn't have worried. The locals have been so welcoming and helpful. They made us feel at home straight away.

Diane Kibbey (WORSTEAD)

This is a wonderful, happy and friendly village. We don't have duck ponds and a green but we do have heart. I have been here about 10 years and retired nearly three years ago when I found there was so much to do it was impossible to take part in everything.

Stella Woods (NECTON)

The view from our shop is timeless. Above the grassy banks sits the castle. Most days it flies the Howard pennant and a family of jackdaws swoop around the stone walls as they probably have done since its most famous resident, Queen Isabella, was kept there in the 1340s. This is a tourist attraction but apart from that, thanks to our squire and landlord Mr. Greville Howard this is also a "living village". As well as myself and the plant centre, he has made it possible for other local businesses to operate in converted buildings. We have a farrier and blacksmith, an art school (West Norfolk Art Centre), a furniture restorer and cabinet maker, a land agents office, a beauty parlour and a thriving local shop and post office. We all support it for stamps, groceries and filled rolls for lunch. Isn't this how a small community should work?

Philip Wing (CASTLE RISING)

A few years ago we had the pleasure of meeting some of the crew of the minesweeper HMS Brinton when they visited the village. Members of the church and Friends of Brinton enjoyed a return visit to go aboard her when she was at Yarmouth.

Joan Croxton (BRINTON)

*Carry on serving … Above, Whissonsett village stores in 1931 with owner
Lawrence Barraclough pictured in the doorway. He and his wife ran the shop from
1929 until 1975. Below, the same shop in 1990, run by Mr. and Mrs. Hall,
pictured in the doorway*

All creatures great and small head for the Worstead Festival each year, one of the most successful in the county. The village throbs with activity.

We came here in 1964 with our two small sons from Cambridge with the Institute of Food Research about to be built at Colney Lane. We soon settled into the village and became involved in many activities. Our children attended the village school and over the years Arnold and I have between us been members, jointly or separately, of the PCC, the parish council, the WI and in the past the village hall committee. I am a churchwarden and my particular interest is church records of the past. Before they were deposited in the Records Office in Bethel Street in Norwich, I spent some time transcribing in date order the disjointed and almost illegible records of births, marriages and deaths of the 18th century. We have a steady trickle of people mainly Australians whose ancestors came from Barford. I have a lot of pleasure in helping to find them, particularly if I can take them back 200 years or more!

Ann Tomalin (BARFORD)

We moved here 22 years ago having purchased two almost-derelict bungalows which we have knocked into one. At the time we had no water or other services and so my husband had to grow a beard. Such newcomers to the village prompted attention and it wasn't long before we had a visit from the local police. It was several years before we discovered why; John Worboys thought we were the Train Robbers and told the police. Yes, we do still speak to him!

Hilary Leighton (BACONSTHORPE)

In the 1930s local residents started what they called the Gymkana Fund. The idea was to raise money and look into the possibility of building a village hall. It took until 1988 for this to become a reality. With the playing field being given to the parish, it seemed sensible to build the hall on the playing field. There were grants from South Norfolk District Council and Norfolk Rural Community Council. The rest of the money came from local organisations and charities and the parish council. Work on the centre was completed in November 1987 by local builder Mr. I. King. It was opened on July 30th, 1988, by Miss Alder Draper, sister of the late William Draper who had contributed so much to the building of the hall. The official name is the William Draper Memorial Hall. The committee consists of a representative from each organisation within the parishes of Dickleburgh and Rushall.

Gerald Seaman (DICKLEBURGH)

Beyond the pail

Sid Plummer was the owner of the night cart and his assistant was William Barnard, known to most as Pokey Dye Barnard. When the council houses were being built at Bradmere Lane it was rumoured that these houses would have an upstairs toilet. This worried William who said to me; "I don't know how old Sid will get on coming down the stairs with the pail; he spills it coming up the garden paths!"

Ted Beales (DOCKING)

Changes

I try to imagine Brockdish
When the loudest noises heard
Were the clip-clop of the horses
Or the mating song of a bird.
Where children could play safely
With hoops or spinning tops,
Where women gossiped on doorsteps
While husbands tended the crops.
Whatever shopping was needed
A shop could supply down The Street,
Fresh baked bread from the baker
And the butcher sold home-killed meat.
There would have been no T.V.
But still there was plenty of fun
Like dances in the village hall
Where hearts were lost and won.
When walking down The Street
It's hard to think of such times
With juggernauts thundering by
And cars in continuous lines.

Eileen Riley (BROCKDISH)

The family seat at the bottom of the garden - but progress has taken Norfolk life beyond the pail!